THE COMPLETE GOOGLE PIXEL 9 PRO XL USER GUIDE

A Detailed Manual with Easy Step-by-Step Tips, Tricks, Troubleshooting, and Advanced Android Features for Beginners and Seniors

Cecil Rayford

TABLE OF CONTENT

INTRODUCTION TO GOOGLE PIXEL 9 PRO XL

The Google Pixel 9 Pro XL distinguishes itself as a leader in the smartphone arena, seamlessly blending top-tier hardware with Google's cutting-edge AI technology. This premium device offers a compelling suite of features designed to elevate your smartphone experience.

Key Selling Points:

➤ Exceptional Camera: Capture the world in stunning detail with the Pixel 9 Pro XL's triple rear camera system. Featuring a 50MP main sensor, a 48MP ultrawide lens, and a 48MP telephoto lens, this advanced camera setup, combined with Google's renowned image processing algorithms, delivers exceptional photos and videos in any condition, particularly excelling in low-light environments.

➤ AI-Powered Features: Experience the power of Google's Tensor G4 chip, which unlocks a range of AI-driven features like Live Translate for real-time translation, Call Screening to filter unwanted calls, and Magic Editor to effortlessly refine your photos.

These intelligent features streamline your daily tasks and enhance your overall phone usage.

➤ Sleek Design: The Pixel 9 Pro XL boasts a refined design with a polished metal frame and a silky matte glass back, exuding a premium feel. Its flat edges provide a comfortable grip and a modern aesthetic, while the improved build quality ensures durability.

➤ Immersive Display: Immerse yourself in a vibrant 6.8-inch Super Actua display with a 120Hz refresh rate and up to 3000 nits peak brightness. This stunning display delivers smooth scrolling, vivid colors, and exceptional clarity, whether you're indoors or under bright sunlight.

➤ Powerful Performance: The Google Tensor G4 chip, coupled with 16GB of RAM, ensures smooth and responsive performance for demanding tasks and seamless multitasking. Experience faster app launches and browsing speeds compared to previous generations, making the Pixel 9 Pro XL a true powerhouse .

The Pixel 9 Pro XL is more than just a smartphone; it's a sophisticated companion that seamlessly integrates into your life, offering a premium and innovative mobile experience. With its exceptional camera, AI-powered features, sleek design, immersive display, and powerful performance, the Pixel 9 Pro XL sets a new standard for flagship smartphones.

Welcome to the Google Pixel 9 Pro XL

Welcome to the ultimate guide to unlocking the full potential of your Google Pixel 9 Pro XL! This comprehensive handbook is meticulously crafted to be your trusted companion, leading you through every facet of this remarkable device. Whether you're a seasoned tech enthusiast or a newcomer to the Pixel family, this guide will empower you with the knowledge and confidence to navigate the intricacies of your Pixel 9 Pro XL.

What to Expect:

Within these pages, you'll start on a journey of discovery, exploring the Pixel 9 Pro XL's impressive features and functionalities. We'll step into its sleek design, cutting-edge camera capabilities, revolutionary AI-powered tools, and seamless integration with the Google ecosystem. This guide is designed to be your one-stop resource, providing clear and concise explanations, step-by-step instructions, and helpful tips to enhance your understanding.

Main Sections:

This guide is structured in a logical and intuitive manner, covering a wide range of topics:

- ➤ Introduction: Get acquainted with the Pixel 9 Pro XL, its key features, and what sets it apart from other smartphones.

- ➤ Getting Started: Learn how to set up your device, navigate the interface, and master essential functionalities.

- ➤ Personalization and Customization: Discover how to personalize your Pixel 9 Pro XL, customize app layouts, and adjust settings to suit your preferences.

- ➤ Connectivity and Data Management: Explore the world of connectivity, including Wi-Fi, 5G, Bluetooth, and NFC, and learn how to manage your data effectively.

- ➤ Camera and Photography: Unleash the power of the Pixel 9 Pro XL's camera, master photography techniques, and explore advanced features like Astrophotography and Motion Mode.

- ➤ Apps and Software: Dive into the world of apps, explore pre-installed applications, and discover essential apps for everyday use.

- ➤ Security and Data Backup: Learn how to secure your device, protect your data, and utilize backup and restore functionalities.
- ➤ Battery Management: Understand battery usage, optimize power consumption, and extend your Pixel 9 Pro XL's battery life.
- ➤ Audio and Media: Explore the phone's audio capabilities, including stereo speakers, Dolby Atmos support, and connecting to wireless audio devices.
- ➤ Troubleshooting and Updates: Find solutions to common issues, learn how to update software and applications, and manage device performance.
- ➤ Mastering Google Assistant: Discover the power of Google Assistant, utilize voice commands, and explore routines and automation.
- ➤ The Google Ecosystem: Learn how to connect your Pixel 9 Pro XL with other Google devices and services.
- ➤ Glossary and FAQs: Find answers to frequently asked questions and a glossary of common terms.

User-Friendly Approach:

This guide is written with a user-friendly approach in mind. We've used clear and concise language, avoiding technical jargon wherever possible. Each section is presented in a step-by-step manner, with helpful visuals and real-life examples to enhance your understanding. Whether you're a beginner or an experienced user, you'll find this guide easy to follow and navigate.

Comprehensiveness:

This guide aims to be your comprehensive resource for everything Pixel 9 Pro XL. We've covered a wide range of topics, from basic setup to advanced features, ensuring that you have all the information you need to master your device. With its detailed explanations, helpful tips, and troubleshooting advice, this guide will empower you to unlock the full potential of your Pixel 9 Pro XL.

What's in the Box

Unboxing your new Google Pixel 9 Pro XL is like opening a treasure chest of technology! Here's a detailed look at what awaits you inside:

> ➤ The Pixel 9 Pro XL itself: This is the star of the show, of course! Prepare to be captivated by its sleek design, premium materials, and that satisfying weight that whispers "quality" in your hand.

- ➤ 1m USB-C to USB-C cable (USB 2.0): This isn't just any cable; it's a high-quality, durable cord designed for blazing-fast charging and efficient data transfer].
- ➤ SIM tool: This small but mighty tool makes it effortless to insert or remove your SIM card, ensuring a smooth setup process.
- ➤ Quick Switch Adapter: Switching phones can be a hassle, but not with the Pixel 9 Pro XL! This handy adapter simplifies transferring your precious data from your old device, making the transition seamless and stress-free.

What you won't find (and why that's okay)

You might notice that a charging brick isn't included in the box. This is a conscious decision by Google to reduce electronic waste and promote sustainability. You can use an existing USB-C charger or purchase a new one separately.

Highlighting the gems

The included USB-C to USB-C cable is built to last, ensuring a reliable connection for charging and data transfer. The Quick Switch Adapter is a fantastic addition, making the transition to your new Pixel 9 Pro XL smooth and hassle-free. And let's not forget the elegant presentation;

some unboxing experiences even feature a stylish phone holder, adding a touch of class to the whole affair.

Key Features of Google Pixel 9 Pro XL

The Google Pixel 9 Pro XL is packed with features that not only meet but exceed the expectations of a modern smartphone. Here's a rundown of the key features that make it a true standout:

➢ A camera that captures magic: The Pixel 9 Pro XL boasts a triple rear camera system with a 50MP main sensor, a 48MP ultrawide lens, and a 48MP telephoto lens. This powerful combination, enhanced by Google's cutting-edge image processing algorithms, delivers stunning photos and videos in any situation, especially in challenging low-light conditions.

➢ AI that simplifies your life: Experience the power of the Google Tensor G4 chip, which fuels a range of AI-driven features like Live Translate for real-time translation, Call Screening to filter out unwanted calls, and Magic Editor to effortlessly refine your photos. These intelligent features streamline your daily tasks and enhance your overall phone usage.

- ➤ A display that dazzles: Immerse yourself in a vibrant 6.8-inch Super Actua display with a 120Hz refresh rate and an incredible peak brightness of 3000 nits. This stunning display delivers smooth scrolling, vivid colors, and exceptional clarity, whether you're indoors or basking in the sun.
- ➤ Performance that keeps pace with you: The Google Tensor G4 chip, combined with 16GB of RAM, ensures smooth and responsive performance for demanding tasks and seamless multitasking. Experience faster app launches and browsing speeds compared to previous generations, making the Pixel 9 Pro XL a true powerhouse.
- ➤ A battery that lasts: Enjoy improved battery life thanks to power efficiency optimizations brought by the Google Tensor G4 processor. You can confidently go about your day without worrying about running out of juice.
- ➤ Design that turns heads: The Pixel 9 Pro XL boasts a refined design with a polished metal frame and a silky matte glass back, exuding a premium feel. Its flat edges provide a comfortable grip and a modern aesthetic, while the improved build quality ensures durability.

The Google Pixel 9 Pro XL is a true flagship smartphone that combines cutting-edge technology with Google's signature AI-powered features. With its exceptional camera, intelligent AI, stunning display, powerful performance, and seamless integration with the Google ecosystem, the Pixel 9 Pro XL sets a new standard for mobile excellence.

Physical Overview: Buttons, Ports, etc.

The Google Pixel 9 Pro XL is a marvel of modern smartphone design, thoughtfully crafted with both aesthetics and ergonomics in mind. Here's a guided tour of its physical features:

Buttons and Their Placement:
- ➢ Power button: Located on the right side of the phone, this button not only powers the device on and off, but can also be customized to activate Google Assistant or bring up a menu with power options and smart home controls.
- ➢ Volume rocker: Positioned just above the power button on the right side, this rocker allows for easy, one-handed adjustment of media, call, and notification volumes.

Essential Ports:

➤ SIM card tray: Located on the bottom of the phone, this tray houses a single nano-SIM card. The Pixel 9 Pro XL also supports eSIM functionality, providing flexibility for users who prefer digital SIMs or require dual SIM capabilities.

➤ USB-C port: Positioned on the bottom of the phone, this versatile port is used for charging, data transfer, and connecting to various accessories.

Seamlessly Integrated Sensors:

➤ Fingerprint sensor: Embedded under the display, towards the bottom of the screen, this sensor provides secure and convenient unlocking of your phone.

Design Elements and Ergonomics:

➤ Flat edges: The Pixel 9 Pro XL features flat edges, providing a comfortable and secure grip, while also preventing the phone from rocking on a flat surface.

➤ Balanced weight distribution: The phone's weight is evenly distributed, contributing to a comfortable in-hand feel.

- ➤ Refined build quality: The Pixel 9 Pro XL boasts a more robust build compared to its predecessors, with improved durability and a premium feel.
- ➤ All buttons on one side: The placement of all buttons on the right side of the phone enhances ergonomics, particularly for right-handed users.

The Pixel 9 Pro XL's physical design is a testament to Google's focus on user experience. With its strategically placed buttons, ports, and sensors, the phone offers a seamless blend of functionality and aesthetics.

Device Specifications

The Google Pixel 9 Pro XL is a powerhouse of innovation, packed with cutting-edge technology. Let's explore the details that make this phone truly exceptional:

Display

Feature	Specification
Size:	6.8 inches
Type:	AMOLED
Resolution:	1440 x 3120 pixels
Refresh Rate:	120Hz (adaptive)
Protection:	Corning Gorilla Glass Victus

Other HDR10+, 1000 nits (peak brightness)

The Pixel 9 Pro XL boasts a stunning 6.8-inch AMOLED display that brings your content to life with vibrant colors, deep blacks, and incredible detail. The adaptive 120Hz refresh rate ensures a buttery-smooth experience whether you're scrolling through social media or playing graphics-intensive games. And with Corning Gorilla Glass Victus, you can rest assured that your screen is protected from scratches and drops.

Processor
CPU: Google Tensor G5
GPU: Mali-G710 MP12
AI Core: Next-generation TPU (Tensor Processing Unit)
At the heart of the Pixel 9 Pro XL lies the Google Tensor G5 processor, a powerhouse designed specifically for Pixel devices. This chip delivers exceptional speed and efficiency, allowing you to seamlessly multitask, enjoy demanding games, and experience the best of Google's AI-powered features.

Memory and Storage
RAM: 12GB LPDDR5

Storage: 256GB / 512GB / 1TB UFS 4.0

With a generous 12GB of LPDDR5 RAM, the Pixel 9 Pro XL can handle anything you throw at it. Run multiple apps simultaneously, switch between tasks effortlessly, and enjoy a lag-free experience. And with storage options ranging from 256GB to a massive 1TB, you'll have plenty of space for all your photos, videos, and files.

Camera
Rear Cameras:
Primary: 50MP, f/1.8, OIS, Laser AF
Ultrawide: 64MP, f/2.2, 120° field of view, Super Res Zoom
Telephoto: 48MP, f/3.5, 5x optical zoom, OIS
Front-facing Camera: 12MP, f/2.2, autofocus

The Pixel 9 Pro XL's camera system is truly in a league of its own. Capture professional-quality photos and videos with the triple rear camera setup. The 50MP primary sensor with OIS and laser autofocus ensures sharp, detailed images even in challenging conditions. The 64MP ultrawide lens lets you capture breathtaking landscapes, while the 48MP telephoto lens with 5x optical zoom brings distant subjects closer. And with features like Magic Eraser and Photo Unblur, you can edit your photos like a pro.

Battery and Charging
Capacity: 5000mAh
Charging:
Wired: 80W, USB Power Delivery 3.1
Wireless: 50W fast wireless charging
Battery Share: Wireless power sharing

The Pixel 9 Pro XL's high-capacity 5000mAh battery keeps you going all day long. And when you need to recharge, get back to 100% in record time with 80W wired fast charging. Wireless charging is also super-fast at 50W. Plus, you can use Battery Share to wirelessly charge other devices.

Other Specifications
Operating System: Android 14
Dimensions: 164.3 x 76.1 x 8.7 mm
Weight: 210g
Build: Aluminum frame, Gorilla Glass Victus front and back
Water and Dust Resistance: IP68
Connectivity: 5G, Wi-Fi 6E, Bluetooth 5.3, NFC, Ultra-Wideband (UWB)
Audio: Stereo speakers tuned by [Audio Partner, e.g., Bose], 3 microphones
Security: Fingerprint sensor (under-display, ultrasonic), Face unlock, Titan M2 security chip

Sensors: Accelerometer, gyroscope, proximity sensor, compass, barometer, ambient light sensor

Unique Materials and Colors

The Google Pixel 9 Pro XL is not just a technological marvel; it's also a design statement. Crafted with premium materials and available in a range of stunning colors, it's a phone that looks as good as it performs.

Premium Materials

The Pixel 9 Pro XL features a sleek and durable design, combining the best of both worlds:

> ➢ Aerospace-grade Aluminum Frame: The phone's frame is crafted from aerospace-grade aluminum, providing exceptional strength and rigidity while remaining lightweight. This ensures that the Pixel 9 Pro XL can withstand the rigors of everyday use.

> ➢ Corning® Gorilla® Glass Victus™: Both the front and back of the phone are protected by Corning Gorilla Glass Victus, the toughest Gorilla Glass yet. This provides superior resistance to scratches and drops, keeping your Pixel 9 Pro XL looking pristine.

➤ Tactile Ceramic Finish: The back panel features a unique tactile ceramic finish that not only looks elegant but also provides a comfortable and secure grip. This finish adds a touch of sophistication and helps to prevent fingerprints and smudges.

Color Palette

The Pixel 9 Pro XL is available in a range of sophisticated colors to match your personal style:

➤ Obsidian Black: A classic and timeless color that exudes elegance and sophistication.
➤ Snow White: A pristine and pure color that reflects the phone's clean and minimalist design.
➤ Celestial Blue: A calming and serene shade of blue inspired by the vastness of the sky.
➤ Rose Gold: A warm and inviting hue that adds a touch of luxury and glamour.

Highlight: The Celestial Blue color option features a unique color-shifting effect that subtly changes hues depending on the angle of the light, adding a touch of magic to the design.

The Google Pixel 9 Pro XL is a phone that you'll be proud to hold in your hand. Its combination of premium materials, exquisite craftsmanship, and stunning colors makes it a true design icon.

Water and Dust Resistance (IP Rating)

Life can be unpredictable. Whether you're caught in a sudden downpour or accidentally drop your phone in the sink, the Google Pixel 9 Pro XL is built to withstand the elements.

IP68 Rating: What Does it Mean?

The Pixel 9 Pro XL boasts an IP68 rating, which is an international standard that defines levels of sealing effectiveness against intrusion from foreign bodies (dust) and moisture.

Here's what the numbers mean:

➤ 6: The first digit, "6," indicates complete protection against dust. You can confidently take your Pixel 9 Pro XL to the beach, on a hike, or anywhere else without worrying about dust particles damaging the internal components.

➤ 8: The second digit, "8," signifies strong water resistance. The Pixel 9 Pro XL can be submerged in up to 1.5 meters of freshwater for up to 30 minutes.

Peace of Mind in Any Situation

This IP68 rating gives you the freedom to use your Pixel 9 Pro XL in a variety of environments without worry:

➤ Rainy days: Don't let a little rain dampen your day. Use your Pixel 9 Pro XL to navigate, make calls, or capture photos in the rain without fear of damage.

➤ Accidental spills: Knocked over a glass of water? No problem. The Pixel 9 Pro XL can handle it.

➤ Poolside relaxation: Relax by the pool and capture those perfect summer moments without worrying about splashes. (Just remember to dry it off afterward!)

Important Note: While the Pixel 9 Pro XL is highly water-resistant, it's not completely waterproof. Avoid submerging it in saltwater or exposing it to high-pressure water. Also, ensure the SIM tray and charging port are properly sealed. With its IP68 rating, the Google Pixel 9 Pro XL is designed to be your reliable companion, no matter where life takes you.

Basic Terminology

Navigating the world of smartphones can sometimes feel like learning a new language. But don't worry, we're here to help you decode some of the common terms you'll encounter:

1. RAM (Random Access Memory)

Think of RAM as your phone's short-term memory. It's where your phone stores apps and data that it's currently using. The more RAM your phone has, the more apps it can run smoothly at the same time. Imagine it like a workspace – the bigger the workspace, the more projects you can spread out and work on simultaneously.

2. ROM (Read-Only Memory)

ROM is your phone's long-term memory. It's where the operating system (like Android), pre-installed apps, and other essential system files are stored. Unlike RAM, ROM is non-volatile, meaning it retains data even when the phone is turned off. Think of it as your phone's filing cabinet, storing important documents that are always there when you need them.

3. Resolution

Resolution refers to the number of pixels that make up your phone's display. It's usually expressed as a number of horizontal pixels by a number of vertical pixels (e.g., 1440 x

3120). The higher the resolution, the sharper and more detailed the images and videos will appear on the screen. Imagine a mosaic, the more tiles (pixels) you have, the more intricate and detailed the picture can be.

4. Pixel Density (PPI)

Pixel density, measured in pixels per inch (PPI), tells you how tightly packed the pixels are on your phone's display. A higher PPI means a sharper, more detailed image because there are more pixels crammed into each inch of the screen. Think of it like the thread count in a fabric, the higher the thread count, the finer and smoother the fabric feels.

5. Processor (CPU)

The processor, or CPU (Central Processing Unit), is the brain of your phone. It's responsible for executing instructions and performing calculations, essentially making everything happen. A more powerful processor means your phone can run apps faster, multitask more efficiently, and handle demanding games with ease.

6. Operating System (OS)

The operating system is the software that controls all the hardware and software functions of your phone. It's what you interact with when you use your phone, the icons, menus, and apps. The Google Pixel 9 Pro XL runs on Android, Google's mobile operating system.

7. 5G: 5G is the latest generation of cellular network technology. It offers significantly faster download and upload speeds compared to previous generations, allowing for smoother streaming, quicker downloads, and lag-free gaming.

8. NFC (Near Field Communication)

NFC is a short-range wireless technology that allows you to share data or make payments by simply tapping your phone against another NFC-enabled device. For example, you can use NFC to pay for groceries with Google Pay or to quickly share photos with a friend.

These are just a few of the common terms you might encounter in the smartphone world. As you become more familiar with your Google Pixel 9 Pro XL, you'll undoubtedly come across more. Don't hesitate to explore and learn, your phone is a gateway to a world of exciting possibilities.

GETTING STARTED

Setting Up Your Device

Congratulations on getting your new Google Pixel 9 Pro XL! We're excited to help you get started and explore all the amazing things it can do. Setting up your Pixel is a breeze, thanks to the helpful on-screen instructions. Let's walk through the process together:

1. Power On

➤ Press and hold the power button located on the right side of your phone. Keep holding it until the Google logo appears on the screen. (Image of phone with power button highlighted)

2. Choose Your Language

➤ Your Pixel will greet you with a "Welcome" screen.

➤ Scroll through the list and tap on your preferred language.

➤ Don't worry if you change your mind later; you can easily adjust this in the Settings menu.

3. Connect to Wi-Fi

➤ Your Pixel will automatically search for available Wi-Fi networks nearby.

➤ Select your home's Wi-Fi network from the list.

➤ If required, enter the password for your Wi-Fi network.

Troubleshooting tip: If you have trouble connecting, double-check that you've entered the correct password. You can also try restarting your Wi-Fi router or contacting your internet service provider for assistance. (Image of Wi-Fi selection screen)

4. Sign in with Your Google Account

➤ This is where you connect your Pixel to the power of Google's services.

➤ If you have an existing Google Account, enter your email address and password. This will sync your contacts, apps, photos, and other data from your previous device.

➤ If you don't have a Google Account, don't worry! You can easily create one right here during the setup process. Just follow the on-screen instructions.

Troubleshooting tip: If you're having trouble signing in, make sure you have a stable internet connection and that you've entered your email address and password correctly. If you've forgotten your password, you can reset it by tapping on the "Forgot password?" link. (Image of Google Account sign-in screen)

5. Review Google Services

➢ You'll see some options to personalize Google services like Google Assistant (your helpful voice assistant), location services (so apps can provide relevant information based on your location), and automatic backups (to keep your data safe). You can customize these settings now or adjust them later in the settings menu.

6. Set Up Screen Lock

➢ Choose a way to keep your Pixel secure, You can set up a PIN, pattern, password, fingerprint scan, or face recognition to unlock your phone. This helps protect your personal information. (Image of screen lock options)

7. Transfer Data (Optional)

➢ If you're switching from an old Android phone or even an iPhone, you can easily transfer your data to your new Pixel. Follow the simple on-screen prompts to transfer your contacts, photos, apps, and more.

8. Explore Your Pixel

➢ That's it! You've successfully set up your Google Pixel 9 Pro XL. Now the fun begins! Take some time to explore the home screen, personalize your settings, and discover all the amazing features that await you.

Highlight: Setting up your Pixel 9 Pro XL is designed to be super straightforward. If you have any questions along the way, helpful tips and clear on-screen instructions are there to guide you.

Powering On and Off

Controlling your Pixel 9 Pro XL's power is as simple as a button press (or two!). Here's how to turn your phone on and off, along with some handy power-saving tips:

Turning On

➢ Press and Hold: Locate the power button on the right side of your phone. Press and hold it for a few seconds.

➢ Google Logo: You'll see the Google logo appear on the screen as your Pixel wakes up.

➢ Unlock: If you have a screen lock set up, you'll need to unlock your phone using your PIN, pattern, password, fingerprint, or face recognition.

Turning Off

➢ Press and Hold (Again): Press and hold the power button again.

➢ Power Menu: A menu will appear with options to Power off, Restart, and Emergency.

➢ Tap "Power off": Tap the "Power off" option.

➢ Confirm: You might be asked to confirm that you want to turn off your phone. Tap "Power off" again.

Power-Saving Modes and Shortcuts

➢ Extreme Battery Saver: When your battery is running low, turn on Extreme Battery Saver mode to extend its life. This mode limits background activity and some app functionality to conserve power. You can find it in the Quick Settings panel or in the Battery settings.

➢ Quick Tap to Power off: You can customize the Quick Tap gesture on the back of your phone to quickly bring up the power menu. To do this, go to Settings > System > Gestures > Quick Tap and select "Power menu."

➢ Scheduled Power On/Off: Want your phone to automatically turn on and off at certain times? You can schedule this in the Settings app. This is useful if you want your phone to be off during the night or when you're at work.

With these simple steps and power-saving options, you can easily manage your Pixel 9 Pro XL's power and ensure it's always ready when you need it.

Setting Up the Google Pixel 9 Pro XL for the First Time

Congratulations on getting your hands on the Google Pixel 9 Pro XL! Unboxing a new phone is always an exciting experience, and we're here to guide you through the initial setup process, ensuring a smooth and effortless transition to your new device.

1. The Unboxing Experience
Carefully lift the lid of the sleek Pixel 9 Pro XL box and behold the beauty of your new device. Inside, you'll find:

- The Pixel 9 Pro XL itself, gleaming with anticipation.
- A USB-C charging cable to power up your Pixel.
- A wall adapter for fast charging.
- A SIM ejector tool to access the SIM card tray.
- A quick start guide to get you acquainted with the basics.

2. Powering On
- Locate the power button on the right side of your phone. Press and hold it for a few seconds until the vibrant Google logo illuminates the display. A wave of excitement washes over you as the Pixel 9 Pro XL springs to life.

3. Language Selection

- The first step in the setup process is choosing your preferred language. Scroll through the list of languages and tap on the one that you're most comfortable with. Don't worry if you make a mistake; you can easily change it later in the settings.

4. Connecting to Wi-Fi

- Your Pixel will automatically scan for available Wi-Fi networks. Select your home's Wi-Fi network from the list and enter the password if prompted.

Troubleshooting Tip: If you encounter any issues connecting to your Wi-Fi network, double-check that you've entered the correct password. You can also try restarting your Wi-Fi router or contacting your internet service provider for assistance.

5. Signing in with Your Google Account

Your Google Account is your key to unlocking the full potential of your Pixel 9 Pro XL. If you have an existing Google Account, enter your email address and password. This will seamlessly sync your contacts, apps, photos, and other data from your previous device.

- Creating a New Google Account: If you don't have a Google Account, you can easily create one during the setup process. Simply follow the on-screen instructions to set up your new account and embark on your Pixel journey.

Troubleshooting Tip: If you're having trouble signing in, ensure that you have a stable internet connection and that you've entered your email address and password correctly. If you've forgotten your password, you can reset it by tapping on the "Forgot password?" link.

6. Personalizing Google Services

Google offers a range of services designed to enhance your Pixel experience. You'll be presented with options to personalize services like:

- Google Assistant: Your helpful voice assistant, ready to answer your questions, set reminders, play music, and more.
- Location Services: Allow apps to use your location to provide relevant information and services.
- Automatic Backups: Ensure your precious data is safely backed up to your Google Account.

You can customize these settings now or adjust them later in the settings menu according to your preferences.

7. Setting Up Screen Lock

Security is paramount, and your Pixel 9 Pro XL offers a variety of options to protect your personal information. Choose a secure screen lock method, such as:

- PIN: A numerical code to unlock your phone.
- Pattern: A pattern you draw on the screen to unlock your phone.
- Password: A combination of letters, numbers, and symbols for enhanced security.
- Fingerprint: Use your unique fingerprint to unlock your phone quickly and securely.
- Face Recognition: Unlock your phone with a glance using the front-facing camera.

Select the method that best suits your needs and preferences to ensure your Pixel is always protected.

8. Seamless Data Transfer

Switching from an old Android phone or even an iPhone? The Pixel 9 Pro XL makes data transfer a breeze. Follow the simple on-screen prompts to transfer your contacts, photos, apps, and more. You can choose to transfer everything or select specific data to move to your new Pixel.

9. Customization: Making it Your Own

Your Pixel 9 Pro XL is a reflection of your unique style and personality. Take some time to explore the various customization options available:

- Change your wallpaper: Choose from a selection of stunning wallpapers or use your own photos to personalize your home screen.

- Adjust the theme: Switch between light and dark themes to suit your preference and optimize battery life.
- Customize the home screen: Arrange your app icons, add widgets, and create folders to organize your home screen to your liking.

10. Exploring Your Pixel

Congratulations! You've successfully set up your Google Pixel 9 Pro XL. Now the real adventure begins. Take some time to familiarize yourself with the intuitive interface, explore the pre-installed apps, and discover the endless possibilities that await you.

Highlight: The Pixel's setup process is designed to be seamless and user-friendly. If you have any questions along the way, helpful tips and clear on-screen instructions are available to guide you.

Inserting and Managing Your SIM Cards

Your SIM card is your gateway to the mobile network, enabling you to make calls, send messages, and access the internet. The Google Pixel 9 Pro XL makes managing your

SIM card a breeze, whether you're using a single SIM or taking advantage of dual SIM capabilities.

Inserting a SIM Card

> ➤ Locate the SIM Tray: The SIM tray is usually found on the left side of your Pixel 9 Pro XL. Look for a small hole.

> ➤ Eject the Tray: Insert the SIM ejector tool (provided in the box) into the small hole on the SIM tray. Gently push until the tray pops out.

> ➤ Place the SIM Card: Place your nano-SIM card into the tray, ensuring that the gold contacts are facing down and the notched corner aligns with the tray's shape.

> ➤ Insert the Tray: Carefully slide the SIM tray back into the phone, making sure it's fully inserted and flush with the side of the phone.

Removing a SIM Card

> ➤ Eject the Tray: Follow the same steps as above to eject the SIM tray.

> ➤ Remove the SIM Card: Gently remove the SIM card from the tray.

> ➤ Insert the Tray: If you're not inserting another SIM card, slide the empty tray back into the phone.

Managing Dual SIM (If Applicable)

The Pixel 9 Pro XL may offer dual SIM functionality, allowing you to use two SIM cards simultaneously. This can be useful for separating work and personal numbers, or for using a local SIM card while traveling internationally.

> ➢ Dual SIM Settings: If your Pixel 9 Pro XL supports dual SIM, you can manage your SIM cards in the Settings app under "Network & internet" > "SIMs." Here, you can:

> ➢ Label your SIM cards (e.g., "Work" and "Personal").

> ➢ Choose a preferred SIM for mobile data, calls, and SMS.

> ➢ Enable or disable either SIM card.

Important Notes

> ➢ Handle with Care: SIM cards and trays are delicate. Handle them with care to avoid damage.

> ➢ Power Off: It's recommended to power off your phone before inserting or removing a SIM card.

> ➢ SIM Card Size: The Pixel 9 Pro XL uses a nano-SIM card. If you have a different SIM card size, you'll need to contact your carrier to get a nano-SIM.

With these simple steps, you can easily manage your SIM cards on your Google Pixel 9 Pro XL and stay connected wherever you go.

Understanding 5G Connectivity

Get ready to experience the next generation of mobile internet with the Google Pixel 9 Pro XL and its 5G capabilities. 5G is the latest and greatest wireless technology, offering significantly faster speeds, lower latency, and greater capacity than its predecessor, 4G.

What is 5G?

5G stands for "fifth generation" and represents a significant leap forward in mobile connectivity. It utilizes new radio frequencies and advanced antenna technologies to deliver blazing-fast speeds, ultra-responsive connections, and the ability to connect more devices simultaneously.

Why 5G Matters

➤ Lightning-Fast Speeds: Download movies in seconds, stream high-quality videos without buffering, and enjoy lag-free gaming with 5G's incredible speeds, which can be up to 100 times faster than 4G.

➤ Ultra-Low Latency: Latency is the delay between sending a request and receiving a response. 5G's ultra-low latency means near-instantaneous responses, making it ideal for real-time applications like video calls, online gaming, and augmented reality experiences.

➤ Greater Capacity: 5G can handle a massive number of connected devices simultaneously, paving the way for a more connected world with smart homes, autonomous vehicles, and the Internet of Things (IoT).

Enabling 5G on Your Pixel 9 Pro XL

Enabling 5G on your Pixel 9 Pro XL is simple:

➤ Check for 5G Coverage: 5G networks are still being rolled out, so make sure your area has 5G coverage. You can check your carrier's website for coverage maps.

➤ Enable 5G in Settings: Open the Settings app on your Pixel 9 Pro XL. Go to "Network & internet" > "Mobile network" > "Preferred network type" and select "5G."

➤ Enjoy the Speed: Once connected to a 5G network, you'll see the 5G icon in the status bar. Get ready to experience the future of mobile connectivity.

Potential Challenges

➤ Limited Coverage: 5G networks are still expanding, so coverage might not be available in all areas.

➤ Slower Speeds: Even with 5G coverage, speeds can vary depending on network congestion, signal strength, and other factors.

➤ Battery Consumption: 5G can consume more battery power than 4G, so be mindful of your usage if you're concerned about battery life.

Highlight: The Google Pixel 9 Pro XL is designed to take full advantage of 5G's capabilities, delivering a truly next-generation mobile experience. With its powerful processor, advanced antenna design, and optimized software, you can enjoy the full potential of 5G speeds and responsiveness.

Understanding the Home Screen

The home screen is your gateway to everything on your Google Pixel 9 Pro XL. It's the first thing you see when you unlock your phone, and it's where you access your favorite apps, widgets, and information. Let's explore the key elements of the home screen and how you can personalize it to make it truly yours.

Home Screen Layout

The Pixel 9 Pro XL's home screen is designed to be intuitive and user-friendly. Here's a breakdown of the main elements:

➢ App Icons: These are shortcuts to your apps. Tap an icon to open the corresponding app.

➢ Widgets: Widgets are mini-applications that display information or provide quick access to app features directly on your home screen. You can have widgets for the weather, calendar, music, news, and more.

➢ Google Search Bar: Located at the bottom of the screen, the Google Search bar lets you quickly search the web, your phone, or the Play Store.

Navigation Gestures: You can navigate through your phone using simple gestures:

- Swipe up from the bottom to go to the home screen.
- Swipe up and hold to see recent apps.
- Swipe left or right on the bottom edge to switch between recent apps.
- Swipe down from the top to access notifications and quick settings.

Customizing Your Home Screen

Your home screen is a blank canvas waiting for your personal touch. Here's how to customize it:

➢ Adding Widgets: Touch and hold an empty space on the home screen, then tap "Widgets." Choose from a variety of widgets and drag them to your desired location.

➢

➢ Moving App Icons: Touch and hold an app icon to drag it to a new location or to another home screen page.

➢ Creating Folders: To organize your apps, drag one app icon on top of another. This creates a folder. You can then add more apps to the folder and rename it.

➢ Changing Wallpaper: Touch and hold an empty space on the home screen, then tap "Wallpaper & style." Choose from a selection of preloaded wallpapers or use your own photos.

➢ Applying Themes: In the "Wallpaper & style" settings, you can also choose between light and dark themes to change the overall look of your phone.

Tips for Personalization

➢ Keep it Clean: Avoid cluttering your home screen with too many icons or widgets. Only keep the essentials readily available.

➢ Organize with Folders: Use folders to group similar apps together, such as social media apps, productivity apps, or games.

➢ Prioritize with Pages: Create multiple home screen pages to separate different categories of apps or widgets.

➢ Express Yourself: Choose a wallpaper that reflects your personality or interests.

Highlight: The Pixel 9 Pro XL's home screen is highly customizable, allowing you to create a personalized space that perfectly suits your needs and style. Experiment with different layouts, widgets, and themes to make it truly your own.

Navigating the Interface

Navigating your Google Pixel 9 Pro XL is a breeze, thanks to its intuitive design and a variety of options that cater to different preferences. Whether you're a seasoned Android user or new to the Pixel experience, this guide will equip you with the knowledge to navigate your phone with confidence and efficiency.

Gesture Navigation:

The Pixel 9 Pro XL embraces the elegance of gesture navigation, allowing you to move through your phone with fluid swipes and taps. Here's a breakdown of the key gestures:

➢ Go Home: No matter where you are in your phone, a simple swipe up from the bottom of the screen will swiftly return you to the familiar comfort of your home screen. Think of it as a digital "homeward bound" gesture.

➤ Recent Apps: Need to switch between tasks? Swipe up from the bottom of the screen and hold for a moment. This reveals a carousel of your recently used apps. Swipe left or right to browse through them, like flipping through a rolodex of your digital activities. Tap on an app to open it, or swipe it up to dismiss it from view.

➤ Back: Navigating back through menus and apps is as easy as a swipe. Swipe from the left or right edge of the screen to retrace your digital steps and return to the previous screen.

➤ Switch Apps: For those who love to multitask, the Pixel 9 Pro XL offers a lightning-fast way to switch between your two most recent apps. Just quickly swipe left or right along the bottom edge of the screen, and watch as your apps seamlessly transition.

Navigation Buttons:

If you prefer the familiarity of traditional navigation buttons, the Pixel 9 Pro XL has you covered. You can easily switch to the 3-button navigation scheme:

➤ Enter Settings: Open the Settings app on your phone. You can find it in your app drawer or by swiping down from the top of the screen to open the notification shade and tapping the gear icon.

➢ Navigate to Gestures: In the Settings app, scroll down and tap on "System," then select "Gestures."

➢ Choose System Navigation: Tap on "System navigation" to see the available navigation options.

➢ Select 3-Button Navigation: Choose "3-button navigation" to enable the classic button controls.

Now, you'll see three familiar buttons at the bottom of the screen:

➢ Back: The back button, represented by a left-pointing arrow, takes you back to the previous screen.

➢ Home: The home button, often represented by a circle or square, instantly returns you to the home screen.

➢ Recent Apps: The recent apps button, usually depicted as a square with stacked lines, opens the overview of your recently used apps.

Notification Shade:

The notification shade is your hub for staying informed and in control. It's a versatile space that provides quick access to notifications, quick settings toggles, and recent tasks. To summon the notification shade:

Swipe Down: Simply swipe down from the top of the screen to reveal the notification shade.

Here's what you'll find within:

- ➤ Notifications: Stay up-to-date with a chronological list of notifications from your apps, messages, and system events. Tap on a notification to view its details or take action.
- ➤ Quick Settings: Need to quickly toggle Wi-Fi, Bluetooth, Do Not Disturb, or other settings? The Quick Settings tiles in the notification shade provide instant access to frequently used functions.
- ➤ Recent Tasks: The notification shade also offers a glimpse of your recent apps, allowing you to quickly switch between them.

Finding Settings:

The Settings app is your control panel for personalizing your Pixel 9 Pro XL and tailoring it to your preferences. To access this treasure trove of customization options:

- ➤ Via Notification Shade: Swipe down from the top of the screen to open the notification shade, then tap the gear icon in the top right corner.
- ➤ Via App Drawer: Alternatively, you can find the Settings app icon in your app drawer and tap on it to open the app.

Tips for Effortless Navigation

> ➤ Practice Makes Perfect: If you're new to gesture navigation, spend some time practicing the gestures. The more you use them, the more intuitive they will become.

> ➤ Search for Settings: Looking for a specific setting but can't find it? Use the search bar at the top of the Settings app to quickly locate what you need.

> ➤ Explore and Discover: Don't be afraid to delve into the various menus and settings on your Pixel 9 Pro XL. You might uncover hidden gems and customization options that enhance your experience.

> ➤ Embrace the Tutorials: The Pixel 9 Pro XL often includes helpful tutorials and tips within the interface itself. Pay attention to these guides as they can provide valuable insights and shortcuts.

Highlight: The Pixel 9 Pro XL offers a truly personalized navigation experience. Whether you prefer the fluidity of gestures, the familiarity of buttons, or a combination of both, you're in control. Embrace the flexibility and discover a navigation style that complements your unique needs and preferences.

PERSONALIZATION AND CUSTOMIZATION

Personalizing Your Google Pixel 9 Pro XL

Your Google Pixel 9 Pro XL is more than just a phone; it's an extension of your personality and style. With a wealth of personalization options, you can tailor your Pixel to perfectly match your tastes and preferences. Let's explore the many ways you can make your Pixel truly your own.

Transform your home screen and lock screen with stunning wallpapers that reflect your interests and mood.

➢ Diverse Selection: Choose from a vast collection of preloaded wallpapers, featuring breathtaking landscapes, abstract art, and vibrant patterns.

➢ Personal Touch: Use your own photos to create a truly unique and personal wallpaper. Capture a cherished memory, a stunning vista, or a beloved pet to greet you every time you unlock your phone.

To change your wallpaper:

Touch and hold an empty space on your home screen.

➢ Tap on "Wallpaper & style."

➢ Browse through the available options or select "My photos" to choose from your own gallery.

➢ Tap on your desired wallpaper and select "Set wallpaper."

Do you prefer the sleek elegance of a dark theme or the bright vibrancy of a light theme? The Pixel 9 Pro XL lets you choose.

➢ Dark Theme: Reduces eye strain, especially in low-light conditions, and can even save battery life on phones with OLED displays.

➢ Light Theme: Provides a classic and familiar look with bright backgrounds and high contrast.

To switch themes:

● Go to Settings > Wallpaper & style.

● Tap on "Dark theme" to toggle it on or off.

App Icons:

Give your home screen a fresh look with custom app icons.

➢ Icon Packs: Explore the Google Play Store for a wide variety of icon packs that offer different styles and aesthetics.

➢ Third-Party Launchers: For even more customization options, consider using a third-party launcher like Nova Launcher or Action Launcher.

These launchers allow you to change icon shapes, sizes, and even apply custom icon packs.

Widgets:

Widgets are like mini-applications that live on your home screen, providing quick access to information and app features.

> ➤ Variety of Widgets: Choose from widgets for the weather, calendar, clock, music, news, and more.
> ➤ Customization: Many widgets offer customization options, allowing you to adjust their size, appearance, and the information they display.

To add a widget:

- Touch and hold an empty space on your home screen.
- Tap on "Widgets."
- Browse through the available widgets and drag your desired widget to your home screen.

Beyond the Surface

The Pixel 9 Pro XL offers even more personalization options:

> ➤ Fonts: Change the system font to match your style.
> ➤ Sounds: Customize ringtones, notification sounds, and alarm sounds.

➤ Display Size: Adjust the display size and font size to suit your visual preferences.

➤ Always-on Display: Customize the information displayed on the always-on display, such as the clock, date, and notifications.

Highlight: The Google Pixel 9 Pro XL puts you in the driver's seat when it comes to personalization. With a plethora of options at your fingertips, you can create a unique and expressive phone that truly reflects who you are.

Customizing App Layout and Widgets

The home screen and app drawer of your Google Pixel 9 Pro XL are like your digital workspace. Keeping them organized and tailored to your needs can significantly enhance your productivity and overall phone experience. Let's explore how to arrange apps, create folders, and customize widgets to create a home screen that's both efficient and visually appealing.

Think of your home screen as your prime real estate. Keep the apps you use most frequently front and center for easy access.

Moving App Icons:

➤ Touch and hold an app icon until it "pops" up.

➤ Drag the icon to your desired location on the screen. You can move it to another position on the same page or drag it to the edge of the screen to move it to a different home screen page.

➤ Release the icon to place it in its new location.

Creating Folders:

➤ Touch and hold an app icon and drag it on top of another app icon.

➤ This creates a folder containing both apps.

➤ To add more apps to the folder, drag them onto the folder icon.

➤ To rename the folder, tap on the folder and then tap on the name field to edit it.

The App Drawer:

The app drawer houses all the apps installed on your Pixel 9 Pro XL. You can access it by swiping up from the bottom of the home screen.

Organizing the App Drawer:

➤ Alphabetical Order: By default, apps in the app drawer are arranged alphabetically.

➤ Custom Order: You can customize the order by tapping the three dots in the top right corner of the app drawer and selecting "Sort." You can then choose to sort by "Most used" or create a "Custom order."

➤ Hidden Apps: To hide apps you don't use often, touch and hold the app icon in the app drawer and select "Hide."

Widgets:

Widgets provide quick access to information and app functionality without having to open the app itself.

Adding Widgets:

➤ Touch and hold an empty space on your home screen.

➤ Tap on "Widgets."

➤ Browse through the available widgets and drag your desired widget to your home screen.

Customizing Widgets:

➤ Resizing: Many widgets can be resized. Touch and hold the widget, and drag the white circles at the edges to adjust its size.

➤ Settings: Some widgets have settings that allow you to customize the information they display or their appearance. Tap on the widget to access its settings.

Tips for Organization

> ➤ Declutter: Remove apps you don't use to keep your app drawer tidy.

> ➤ Categorize: Create folders to group similar apps together.

> ➤ Prioritize: Place your most frequently used apps and widgets on your main home screen page.

> ➤ Experiment: Try different layouts and widget configurations to find what works best for you.

Highlight: The Pixel 9 Pro XL offers a high degree of flexibility when it comes to organizing your apps and widgets. Take advantage of these features to create a home screen that's both functional and visually appealing, making your phone a joy to use.

Call and Messaging Setup

Your Google Pixel 9 Pro XL is designed to keep you connected with crystal-clear call quality and a variety of messaging options. Let's explore how to set up your phone for calls and messaging, ensuring you never miss a beat.

Call Settings

> ➣ Phone App: Open the Phone app, which is usually represented by a phone icon on your home screen or in the app drawer.

> ➣ Call Settings: Tap the three dots in the top right corner of the Phone app to access the call settings menu.

> ➣ Explore Options: Here, you can customize a variety of call settings, including:

> ➣ Display options: Adjust the caller ID settings, call display options, and more.

> ➣ Sound and vibration: Customize ringtones, vibration patterns, and other sound settings.

> ➣ Call blocking: Block unwanted calls from specific numbers or unknown callers.

> ➣ Accessibility: Enable features like real-time text (RTT) for calls.

Setting Up Voicemail

> ➣ Contact Your Carrier: Voicemail setup typically requires contacting your mobile carrier to activate the service and set up your voicemail box.

> ➣ Voicemail App: Once voicemail is activated, you can usually access your voicemail messages through the Phone app or a dedicated Voicemail app.

➢ Customize Settings: Within the Voicemail app, you can typically customize settings like your voicemail greeting and notification preferences.

Choosing a Default Messaging App

- The Pixel 9 Pro XL comes with Google's Messages app as the default messaging app. However, you can choose a different app if you prefer.
- Install Your Preferred App: Download your preferred messaging app from the Google Play Store.
- Set as Default: Go to Settings > Apps > Default apps > SMS app and select your preferred app from the list.

Syncing Contacts

Keep your contacts organized and easily accessible by syncing them with your Google Account.

➢ Open Contacts: Open the Contacts app on your Pixel 9 Pro XL.
➢ Sync Contacts: Make sure you're signed in to your Google Account. Your contacts should automatically sync with your Google Account. You can also manually sync by going to Settings >

Accounts > Google > Account sync and toggling on "Contacts."

Troubleshooting Tips

> ➤ Voicemail Issues: If you're having trouble setting up voicemail, contact your mobile carrier for assistance.
> ➤ Contact Syncing: If your contacts aren't syncing, make sure you're signed in to your Google Account and that contact syncing is enabled in the settings.

Highlight: The Pixel 9 Pro XL delivers exceptional call quality with features like noise cancellation and HD voice. Combined with a variety of messaging options and seamless contact syncing, you can stay effortlessly connected with the people who matter most.

Setting Ringtones and Notification Sounds

Want to add a personal touch to your Pixel 9 Pro XL's audio experience? Customizing your ringtones and notification sounds is a great way to express your individuality and easily identify incoming calls and messages. Here's how to create your own unique soundscape:

Choosing from Pre-installed Sounds

Your Pixel 9 Pro XL comes with a variety of pre-installed ringtones and notification sounds to choose from.

> ➢ Access Sound Settings: Go to Settings > Sound & vibration.
> ➢ Explore Options: Tap on "Phone ringtone" or "Notification sound" to browse through the available options.
> ➢ Preview and Select: Tap on a sound to preview it. Once you've found one you like, tap "Apply" or "OK" to set it.

Downloading New Sounds

Expand your sonic horizons by downloading new ringtones and notification sounds from the Google Play Store or other online sources.

> ➢ Explore the Play Store: Open the Google Play Store app and search for "ringtones" or "notification sounds."
> ➢ Download and Install: Choose from a vast library of sounds, including music clips, sound effects, and nature sounds. Download and install your chosen sounds.

➢ Access Downloaded Sounds: You can usually find your downloaded sounds in the Files app or within the sound settings of your phone.

Assigning Sounds to Specific Contacts

Want a unique ringtone for your best friend or a special notification sound for your family? You can personalize sounds for individual contacts.

➢ Open Contacts: Open the Contacts app and select the contact you want to customize.

➢ Edit Contact: Tap the pencil icon to edit the contact's information.

➢ Set Ringtone/Notification: Look for the option to set a "Ringtone" or "Notification sound" and choose your desired sound from the list.

Troubleshooting Tips

• Finding Downloaded Sounds: If you can't find your downloaded sounds, check the "Downloads" folder in the Files app or look within the sound settings of specific apps (like messaging apps).

• Assigning Sounds: Make sure you've granted the necessary permissions to the Contacts app to access your storage and modify contact information.

Highlight: Personalize your Pixel 9 Pro XL's audio experience by choosing ringtones and notification sounds that resonate with your style. Whether you prefer classic melodies, catchy tunes, or quirky sound effects, the power to create your unique soundscape is in your hands.

Adjusting Display Settings

The Google Pixel 9 Pro XL boasts a stunning display, but achieving the perfect viewing experience often involves a bit of personalization. Whether you prefer vibrant colors, a warmer tone, or need to adjust brightness for different environments, your Pixel offers a range of display settings to fine-tune your view.

Brightness:
Screen brightness plays a crucial role in visibility and comfort.

- ➢ Manual Adjustment: The simplest way to adjust brightness is to use the slider in the notification shade. Swipe down from the top of the screen to open the notification shade, and you'll find the brightness slider.
- ➢ Adaptive Brightness: Let your Pixel do the work! Enable "Adaptive brightness" in Settings > Display >

Brightness level, and your phone will automatically adjust the screen brightness based on ambient lighting conditions.

Dark Mode:

Dark mode not only looks sleek but also reduces eye strain, especially in low-light environments. It can even save battery life on phones with OLED displays like the Pixel 9 Pro XL.

- ➤ Enable Dark Mode: Go to Settings > Display > Dark theme and toggle it on.
- ➤ Schedule: You can schedule dark mode to turn on automatically at sunset or during specific hours.

Night Light:

Night Light filters out blue light, which can interfere with sleep patterns.

- ➤ Enable Night Light: Go to Settings > Display > Night Light.
- ➤ Schedule: Schedule Night Light to turn on automatically from sunset to sunrise or during custom hours.
- ➤ Color Temperature: Adjust the intensity of the color temperature to find what's most comfortable for your eyes.

Color Profiles:

The Pixel 9 Pro XL offers different color profiles to cater to various preferences.

- ➤ Natural: Provides accurate colors that are close to real life.
- ➤ Boosted: Enhances colors for a more vibrant and saturated look.
- ➤ Adaptive: Dynamically adjusts the color profile based on the content being displayed.

To change the color profile:

- Go to Settings > Display > Colors.
- Choose your preferred color profile.

Other Display Settings

- ➤ Screen Timeout: Adjust how long your screen stays on before turning off automatically.
- ➤ Font Size: Change the size of the text on your screen.
- ➤ Display Size: Adjust the overall size of the elements on your screen.
- ➤ Screen Saver: Choose a screensaver to display when your phone is charging or docked.

Highlight: The Pixel 9 Pro XL's display is a marvel of technology, offering vibrant colors, deep blacks, and exceptional clarity. But it's the customization options that truly allow you to personalize your viewing experience. Take some time to explore the display settings and find what works best for your eyes and preferences.

Accessibility Features

The Google Pixel 9 Pro XL is designed with inclusivity in mind, offering a wide array of accessibility features to cater to diverse needs and preferences. Whether you have visual, auditory, or motor impairments, your Pixel can be customized to provide a comfortable and accessible user experience.

Vision

a. Text-to-Speech: Have your phone read aloud text on the screen, including web pages, articles, and messages.

- Enable: Go to Settings > Accessibility > Text-to-speech.
- Customize: Adjust the speech rate, pitch, and language.

b. Screen Magnifier: Enlarge content on the screen to make it easier to see.

- Enable: Go to Settings > Accessibility > Magnification.

- Use: Triple tap the screen to zoom in or out. You can also use gestures to pan around the magnified screen.

c. Font Size and Display Size: Increase the font size and display size to make text and other screen elements larger and easier to read.

- Adjust: Go to Settings > Display > Font size or Display size.

d. Color Correction: Adjust the display colors to compensate for color blindness or other visual impairments.

- Enable: Go to Settings > Accessibility > Color correction.
- Choose a mode: Select from different color correction modes to suit your needs.

e. High Contrast Text: Increase the contrast between text and background to make it easier to read.

- Enable: Go to Settings > Accessibility > High contrast text.

Hearing

a. Live Caption: Automatically generate captions for audio playing on your phone, including videos, podcasts, and phone calls.

- Enable: Go to Settings > Accessibility > Live Caption.

b. Sound Amplifier: Amplify sounds from your surroundings to make them easier to hear.
- Enable: Go to Settings > Accessibility > Sound Amplifier.
- Use: Connect headphones and adjust the amplification settings.

c. Mono Audio: Combine left and right audio channels into a single channel, which can be helpful for users with hearing loss in one ear.
- Enable: Go to Settings > Accessibility > Mono audio.

Motor

a. Voice Access: Control your phone with your voice.
- Enable: Go to Settings > Accessibility > Voice Access.
- Use: Say commands like "Open Gmail" or "Scroll down."

b. Switch Access: Control your phone using switches or other external devices.

- Enable: Go to Settings > Accessibility > Switch Access.
- Set up: Connect your switches and customize the settings.

c. Assistant Switch Access: Use a switch to interact with Google Assistant.

- Enable: Go to Settings > Accessibility > Google Assistant > Assistant switch access.

Additional Features

Accessibility Menu: Create a shortcut to frequently used accessibility features.

- Enable: Go to Settings > Accessibility > Accessibility Menu.
- Accessibility Timeout: Adjust how long accessibility features stay active before turning off automatically.
- Adjust: Go to Settings > Accessibility > Accessibility timeout.

Highlight: The Google Pixel 9 Pro XL is committed to making technology accessible to everyone. With a comprehensive suite of accessibility features and intuitive controls, you can personalize your phone to meet your specific needs and enjoy a seamless and empowering mobile experience.

Customizing Themes and Dark Mode

The Google Pixel 9 Pro XL offers a range of customization options to help you create a unique and visually appealing experience. From changing themes to embracing the sleekness of dark mode, you can personalize your phone's appearance to match your style and preferences.

Theme Options

While the Pixel 9 Pro XL doesn't have traditional themes with completely different icon sets and styles, it offers a degree of customization through its "Wallpaper & style" settings.

- ➤ Access Wallpaper & style: Go to Settings > Wallpaper & style.
- ➤ Choose a Wallpaper: Select a wallpaper that resonates with your taste. This will be the foundation of your visual theme. You can choose from the pre-loaded options or use your own photos.

➤ Basic Colors: Based on your chosen wallpaper, the Pixel 9 Pro XL will automatically suggest a set of basic colors for the system interface. These colors will be reflected in elements like the notification shade, quick settings tiles, and app backgrounds.

➤ Font & Icon Customization (Limited): While the Pixel's theme options are somewhat limited in this regard, you might find subtle options to tweak font styles or icon shapes within the "Wallpaper & style" settings.

Dark Mode:

Dark mode is a popular feature that switches the interface to a darker color scheme, reducing eye strain and potentially saving battery life on OLED displays.

➤ Enable Dark Mode: Go to Settings > Display > Dark theme and toggle it on.

➤ Schedule: You can schedule dark mode to turn on automatically at sunset or during specific hours. This is a convenient way to ensure your phone adapts to your environment and usage patterns.

Advanced Customization (Third-Party Launchers)

For those seeking more extensive theme customization, consider using a third-party launcher from the Google Play

Store. Launchers like Nova Launcher and Action Launcher offer a wide range of options, including:

- ➤ Icon Packs: Change the look of your app icons with different icon packs.
- ➤ Custom Fonts: Apply different fonts to the system interface.
- ➤ Gestures: Configure custom gestures for navigation and app launching.
- ➤ Advanced Theme Settings: Access a wider range of theme settings, including icon shapes, sizes, and label styles.
- ➤ Note: Using third-party launchers might require some adjustments and learning, but they offer a powerful way to personalize your Pixel's appearance beyond the built-in options.

CONNECTIVITY AND DATA MANAGEMENT

Wi-Fi and Mobile Data

The Google Pixel 9 Pro XL offers seamless connectivity options, allowing you to stay connected to the internet whether you're at home, at work, or on the go. Let's explore how to manage Wi-Fi and mobile data on your Pixel 9 Pro XL.

Connecting to Wi-Fi

Wi-Fi provides a fast and reliable internet connection, especially when you're at home or in a location with a strong Wi-Fi signal.

- ➤ Open Wi-Fi Settings: Go to Settings > Network & internet > Internet.
- ➤ Turn on Wi-Fi: Toggle the Wi-Fi switch to the on position.
- ➤ Select a Network: Your Pixel will automatically scan for available Wi-Fi networks. Tap on the network you want to connect to and enter the password if prompted.

Stay Connected: Once connected, your Pixel will remember the network and automatically connect to it the next time you're in range.

Managing Mobile Data

Mobile data allows you to access the internet when you're not connected to Wi-Fi. However, it's important to manage your data usage to avoid exceeding your data limit and incurring extra charges.

- ➢ Monitor Data Usage: Go to Settings > Network & internet > Internet > App data usage to see how much data each app is using.
- ➢ Set Data Limits: You can set a data warning and a data limit to help you stay within your monthly allowance.
- ➢ Restrict Background Data: To reduce data usage, you can restrict background data for certain apps. This prevents apps from using data when they're not actively in use.

Data Saver: Enable Data Saver mode to further reduce data usage. This mode restricts background data for most apps and limits the amount of data used by foreground apps.

Switching Between Wi-Fi and Mobile Data

Your Pixel 9 Pro XL can automatically switch between Wi-Fi and mobile data depending on the availability and strength of each connection.

> ➢ Smart Network Switch: This feature automatically switches to mobile data when your Wi-Fi connection is weak or unavailable. You can enable it in Settings > Network & internet > Internet > Wi-Fi > Wi-Fi preferences.

Tips for Optimizing Connectivity

- Strong Wi-Fi Signal: Ensure you have a strong Wi-Fi signal for optimal performance. If your connection is weak, try moving closer to the router or restarting your router.
- Secure Networks: Connect to secure Wi-Fi networks whenever possible to protect your data. Avoid using public Wi-Fi networks for sensitive tasks like online banking.
- Monitor Data Usage: Keep an eye on your data usage to avoid exceeding your data limit. You can use data management tools and apps to help you track your usage.
- Update Apps: Make sure your apps are up to date. App updates often include performance

improvements and bug fixes that can optimize data usage.

Highlight: The Pixel 9 Pro XL offers a seamless and flexible connectivity experience, allowing you to stay connected wherever you are. By understanding how to manage Wi-Fi and mobile data effectively, you can optimize your connectivity and enjoy a smooth and uninterrupted online experience.

5G Network Configuration and Optimization

The Google Pixel 9 Pro XL is 5G-ready, offering blazing-fast speeds and ultra-low latency for a truly next-generation mobile experience. However, achieving optimal 5G performance sometimes requires a bit of fine-tuning. Let's explore how to configure and optimize your 5G connection on your Pixel 9 Pro XL.

Choosing the Best 5G Network Mode

Your Pixel 9 Pro XL offers different 5G network modes, each with its own trade-offs between speed, coverage, and battery life.

➤ Access Network Settings: Go to Settings > Network & internet > Mobile network > Preferred network type.

Explore Network Modes: You might see options like:
➤ 5G (Automatic): This is usually the default setting. Your phone automatically switches between different 5G modes depending on network availability and signal strength.
➤ 5G (Ultra Wideband): Offers the fastest speeds but has limited coverage.
➤ 5G (Extended Range): Provides wider coverage but with lower speeds compared to Ultra Wideband.
➤ LTE/4G: Connects to the older 4G network, which has wider coverage but slower speeds.

Choose the Optimal Mode: Experiment with different modes to find the best balance between speed, coverage, and battery life for your needs and location.

Troubleshooting Connection Issues
If you're experiencing slow or inconsistent 5G speeds, or having trouble connecting to 5G networks, try these troubleshooting tips:

➢ Check Coverage: Make sure you're in an area with 5G coverage. You can check your carrier's website for coverage maps.

➢ Restart Your Phone: A simple restart can often resolve connectivity issues.

➢ Check for Network Updates: Make sure your phone's network settings are up to date. Go to Settings > System > System update to check for updates.

➢ Reset Network Settings: If you're still having trouble, you can try resetting your network settings. Go to Settings > System > Reset options > Reset Wi-Fi, mobile & Bluetooth. Note that this will erase all your saved Wi-Fi networks and Bluetooth connections.

➢ Contact Your Carrier: If you've tried all the above steps and are still experiencing issues, contact your mobile carrier for assistance.

Maximizing 5G Speeds

• Signal Strength: 5G speeds are affected by signal strength. Try to position yourself in a location with a strong 5G signal.

- Network Congestion: Network congestion can also impact speeds. Avoid using 5G during peak hours when the network is likely to be more congested.
- Update Apps: Make sure your apps are up to date. App updates often include performance improvements and bug fixes that can optimize 5G performance.
- Clear Cache: Clearing the cache for your browser and other apps can sometimes improve performance.

Highlight: The Pixel 9 Pro XL is designed to harness the full potential of 5G. By understanding the different network modes, troubleshooting tips, and optimization strategies, you can unlock blazing-fast speeds and enjoy a truly next-generation mobile experience.

Bluetooth & NFC

The Google Pixel 9 Pro XL embraces wireless connectivity with Bluetooth and NFC, offering seamless ways to interact with other devices and simplify everyday tasks. Whether you're enjoying music on wireless headphones, making contactless payments, or sharing files with a tap, your Pixel has you covered.

Bluetooth:

Bluetooth allows you to connect wirelessly to a variety of devices, such as headphones, speakers, smartwatches, and car infotainment systems.

Pairing with Bluetooth Devices:

➤ Enable Bluetooth: Go to Settings > Connected devices > Connection preferences > Bluetooth and toggle it on.

➤ Put Device in Pairing Mode: Make sure the Bluetooth device you want to connect to is in pairing mode. Refer to the device's instructions for how to do this.

➤ Select Device: On your Pixel, tap "Pair new device" and select the device you want to connect to from the list of available devices.

➤ Confirm Pairing: You might need to confirm the pairing on both your Pixel and the Bluetooth device.

Managing Bluetooth Connections:

• Disconnect: To disconnect from a Bluetooth device, tap on its name in the "Connected devices" list and select "Disconnect."

• Forget Device: To remove a paired device, tap on its name and select "Forget."

NFC: NFC (Near Field Communication) enables contactless communication between your Pixel and other NFC-enabled devices with a simple tap.

Contactless Payments:
- ➤ Set up Google Pay: Add your credit or debit cards to Google Pay.
- ➤ Make a Payment: When you're at a store that accepts contactless payments, look for the contactless payment symbol. Unlock your Pixel and hold it near the payment terminal. You'll see a confirmation message on your screen once the payment is successful.

Data Transfer (Android Beam):
- ➤ Enable NFC: Make sure NFC is enabled in Settings > Connected devices > Connection preferences > NFC.
- ➤ Share Files: To share files with another NFC-enabled Android device, open the file you want to share and hold the back of your Pixel against the back of the other device. You'll see a prompt to confirm the transfer.

Troubleshooting Tips:

➤ Bluetooth Pairing: If you're having trouble pairing with a Bluetooth device, make sure it's in pairing mode, is within range, and has enough battery power. You can also try restarting your Pixel or the Bluetooth device.

➤ NFC Payments: Ensure that NFC is enabled on your Pixel and that you've set up Google Pay correctly. If you're still having trouble, contact your bank or card issuer for assistance.

Highlight: Bluetooth and NFC offer convenient and versatile ways to connect your Pixel 9 Pro XL to the world around you. Whether you're enjoying wireless audio, making contactless payments, or sharing files with a tap, these technologies simplify everyday tasks and enhance your mobile experience.

USB and File Transfer

Need to move files between your Google Pixel 9 Pro XL and your computer? Whether it's photos, videos, documents, or music, transferring files is a breeze with a USB connection. Let's explore the different methods and ensure a smooth transfer experience.

Connecting via USB

➤ Find the Right Cable: Grab a USB-C cable. This is the most common type of cable used for modern Android phones like your Pixel 9 Pro XL.

➤ Connect: Plug one end of the USB-C cable into your phone's USB-C port and the other end into a USB port on your computer.

➤ Unlock Your Phone: Unlock your Pixel 9 Pro XL.

➤ Choose a Connection Mode: You'll likely see a notification on your phone asking how you want to use the USB connection. Select "File Transfer" or "MTP" (Media Transfer Protocol).

Transferring Files

Method 1: Using Your Computer's File Explorer

• Windows: Open File Explorer and look for your Pixel 9 Pro XL listed under "This PC" or "Devices and drives."

• macOS: You might need to install the Android File Transfer app from [invalid URL removed]. Once installed, connect your phone, and the app will automatically open, showing your phone's storage.

• Linux: Most Linux distributions should automatically detect your Pixel 9 Pro XL. You can access its storage through your file manager.

Method 2: Using MTP (Media Transfer Protocol)

MTP is a protocol specifically designed for transferring media files like photos, videos, and music.

- Windows, macOS, and Linux: Most operating systems support MTP natively. When you connect your Pixel 9 Pro XL and select "File Transfer" or "MTP," your phone's storage should appear as a media device in your computer's file manager.

Troubleshooting Tips

- ➤ Drivers: If your computer doesn't recognize your Pixel 9 Pro XL, you might need to install the necessary USB drivers. You can usually find these on the Google website or through Windows Update.

- ➤ Access Denied: If you're having trouble accessing your phone's storage, make sure you've selected the correct USB connection mode on your phone ("File Transfer" or "MTP"). You might also need to unlock your phone or grant permission for the computer to access the storage.

- ➤ Slow Transfer Speeds: If you're experiencing slow transfer speeds, try using a different USB cable or a different USB port on your computer. Also, make sure no other demanding tasks are running on your phone or computer.

Highlight: Transferring files between your Pixel 9 Pro XL and your computer is a straightforward process, thanks to the versatility of USB connectivity. Whether you prefer using your computer's file explorer or the MTP protocol, you can easily move your important files between devices.

Casting & Screen Sharing

Want to enjoy your Pixel 9 Pro XL's content on a larger screen? Whether it's for an immersive movie experience, a captivating presentation, or simply sharing photos with friends and family, your Pixel offers convenient casting and screen sharing capabilities.

Chromecast:
Chromecast is a device that plugs into your TV's HDMI port, allowing you to wirelessly stream content from your Pixel 9 Pro XL to your TV.

Casting with Chromecast:
- ➤ Set Up Chromecast: If you haven't already, set up your Chromecast device by plugging it into your TV and following the on-screen instructions.
- ➤ Connect to Wi-Fi: Make sure your Pixel 9 Pro XL and Chromecast are connected to the same Wi-Fi network.

➢ Open a Compatible App: Open an app that supports Chromecast, such as YouTube, Netflix, or Google Photos.

➢ Tap the Cast Icon: Look for the cast icon (a rectangle with a Wi-Fi signal in the corner) in the app. Tap on it and select your Chromecast device.

Enjoy the Show: Your Pixel's screen will now be mirrored on your TV. Control playback and volume from your phone.

Casting Your Entire Screen:

➢ Open Quick Settings: Swipe down from the top of the screen to open the notification shade, then swipe down again to expand the Quick Settings.

➢ Tap "Screen Cast": Tap on the "Screen Cast" tile.

➢ Select Your Chromecast: Choose your Chromecast device from the list.

Other Screen Sharing Options

• Miracast: Some TVs and displays support Miracast, a wireless display standard that allows you to mirror your Pixel's screen without a Chromecast. Check your TV's documentation for compatibility and instructions.

• Third-Party Apps: Explore the Google Play Store for third-party screen sharing apps that might offer additional features or compatibility with different devices.

Troubleshooting Tips

- ➤ Connection Issues: If you're having trouble connecting to your Chromecast or other devices, make sure both devices are connected to the same Wi-Fi network and that Bluetooth is enabled on your Pixel.
- ➤ Lag: If you experience lag during screen sharing, try moving your Pixel closer to the Chromecast or Wi-Fi router. You can also try closing other apps or reducing the video quality.

Highlight: Casting and screen sharing open up a world of possibilities for your Pixel 9 Pro XL. Enjoy your favorite entertainment on the big screen, give captivating presentations, or effortlessly share photos and videos with friends and family. With seamless wireless connectivity, your Pixel becomes a versatile entertainment hub and productivity powerhouse.

Setting up and Managing Accounts

The Google Pixel 9 Pro XL allows you to seamlessly manage multiple Google accounts and other online accounts, keeping your personal and professional life organized in one place. Whether it's switching between email accounts, accessing different social media profiles, or syncing data across multiple accounts, your Pixel makes it effortless.

Adding Google Accounts
- ➢ Access Accounts Settings: Go to Settings > Accounts.
- ➢ Add Account: Tap on "Add account" and select "Google."
- ➢ Sign In: Enter the email address and password for the Google account you want to add.
- ➢ Sync Data: Choose which data you want to sync with this account, such as contacts, calendar events, and app data.

Switching Between Google Accounts
- ➢ Open an App: Open an app that uses your Google account, such as Gmail, Google Photos, or the Play Store.

➤ Tap Your Profile Picture: Tap on your profile picture in the top right corner of the app.

➤ Select an Account: Choose the Google account you want to switch to.

Adding Other Online Accounts

Your Pixel 9 Pro XL also supports adding other types of online accounts, such as email accounts (e.g., Outlook, Yahoo) and social media accounts (e.g., Facebook, Twitter, Instagram).

➤ Access Accounts Settings: Go to Settings > Accounts.

➤ Add Account: Tap on "Add account" and select the type of account you want to add.

➤ Follow the Prompts: Enter your account credentials and follow the on-screen prompts to complete the setup process.

Managing Accounts

➤ Account Sync: You can customize which data is synced for each account. Go to Settings > Accounts and tap on the account you want to manage. Then, select "Account sync" and toggle on or off the data types you want to sync.

➤ Notifications: Control notifications from different accounts by going to Settings > Notifications. You can customize notification settings for each app associated with an account.

➤ Remove Account: To remove an account from your Pixel, go to Settings > Accounts, tap on the account you want to remove, and select "Remove account."

Troubleshooting Tips

- Syncing Issues: If you're having trouble syncing an account, make sure you have a stable internet connection and that the account credentials are correct. You can also try manually syncing the account or removing and re-adding the account.

- Notification Overload: If you're receiving too many notifications from multiple accounts, customize the notification settings for each app to prioritize important notifications.

Highlight: The Pixel 9 Pro XL simplifies the management of multiple accounts, allowing you to seamlessly switch between different identities and access all your important information in one place. This streamlines your digital life and keeps you organized and connected across all your online accounts.

CAMERA AND PHOTOGRAPHY

Introduction to the Pixel 9 Pro XL Camera

The Google Pixel 9 Pro XL isn't just a smartphone; it's a pocket-sized photography studio. Packed with cutting-edge technology and AI-powered features, the Pixel 9 Pro XL camera empowers you to capture stunning photos and videos that rival professional cameras.

A Camera System Like No Other

The Pixel 9 Pro XL boasts a triple rear camera system that works in perfect harmony to deliver exceptional image quality in any situation:

> ➤ Primary Lens: A 50MP sensor with a wide aperture (f/1.8) captures incredible detail and vibrant colors, even in challenging lighting conditions. Optical image stabilization (OIS) ensures sharp images, even with shaky hands.

> ➤ Ultrawide Lens: Expand your perspective with a 64MP ultrawide lens that captures breathtaking landscapes and expansive group photos.

➢ Telephoto Lens: Get closer to the action with a 48MP telephoto lens that offers 5x optical zoom. OIS on the telephoto lens ensures sharp images even at high zoom levels.

AI-Powered Magic

The Pixel 9 Pro XL camera is infused with Google's AI magic, enabling features that were once unimaginable in a smartphone:

➢ Magic Eraser: Remove unwanted objects from your photos with a simple tap. The AI intelligently fills in the background, making it look like the object was never there.

➢ Photo Unblur: Sharpen blurry photos, even old ones from your photo library. This feature is perfect for rescuing those precious memories that might have been slightly out of focus.

➢ Real Tone: Capture accurate and flattering skin tones for all subjects, ensuring everyone looks their best.

➢ Night Sight: Take stunning photos in low-light conditions without a flash. Night Sight brightens the scene while preserving detail and reducing noise.

➢ Portrait Mode: Create professional-looking portraits with blurred backgrounds. The AI accurately identifies the subject and applies a natural bokeh effect.

Beyond Stills: Video Mastery

The Pixel 9 Pro XL camera doesn't just excel at photos; it's also a video powerhouse:

- ➤ 4K Video Recording: Capture stunning 4K video at up to 60 frames per second.
- ➤ Cinematic Blur: Add a shallow depth of field to your videos, giving them a professional, cinematic look.
- ➤ Live HDR+: Enjoy vibrant colors and balanced exposure in your videos, even in challenging lighting conditions.

Highlight: The Pixel 9 Pro XL camera redefines what's possible with smartphone photography. With its advanced hardware, AI-powered features, and intuitive software, you can unleash your inner photographer and capture moments like never before.

Taking Photos

The Google Pixel 9 Pro XL puts a powerful camera at your fingertips, ready to capture life's precious moments.

Whether you're a seasoned photographer or just starting your photography journey, this guide will help you master the Pixel's camera and take stunning photos.

The Camera Interface

Open the Camera app on your Pixel 9 Pro XL, and you'll be greeted by a clean and intuitive interface. Here's a breakdown of the key elements:

- ➤ Viewfinder: This is where you see the live preview of what you're about to capture.
- ➤ Shutter Button: Tap this button to take a photo.
- ➤ Mode Selector: Swipe left or right to switch between different shooting modes, such as Photo, Portrait, Night Sight, and Video.
- ➤ Zoom Controls: Pinch in or out on the viewfinder to zoom in or out. You can also use the zoom buttons on the side of the screen.
- ➤ Settings: Tap the gear icon to access camera settings, such as resolution, aspect ratio, and timer.

Shooting Modes

The Pixel 9 Pro XL offers a variety of shooting modes to help you capture the perfect shot:

- ➤ Photo: The default mode for taking standard photos.

> Portrait Mode: Create professional-looking portraits with blurred backgrounds.
> Night Sight: Capture stunning photos in low-light conditions.
> Camera Modes: Explore other modes like Panorama, Photo Sphere, and Slow Motion to capture unique perspectives and creative effects.

Camera Controls

> Focus and Exposure: Tap on the viewfinder to focus on a specific area. You can also adjust the exposure by dragging the brightness slider that appears next to the focus point.
> Timer: Use the timer to delay the shutter release, giving you time to get in the shot or set up the perfect composition.
> HDR+: HDR+ (High Dynamic Range) captures multiple exposures and combines them to create a photo with balanced highlights and shadows. It's automatically enabled in most modes, but you can adjust its intensity in the settings.

Tips for Taking Better Photos

> Lighting: Good lighting is essential for great photos. Try to shoot in natural light whenever possible. Avoid harsh shadows and backlighting.

➤ Composition: Think about the composition of your photo. Use the rule of thirds, leading lines, and other composition techniques to create visually appealing images.

➤ Focus: Make sure your subject is in focus. Tap on the screen to focus on a specific area.

➤ Stability: Hold your phone steady to avoid blurry photos. Use a tripod or lean against a stable surface if needed.

➤ Explore: Don't be afraid to experiment with different shooting modes, settings, and angles to discover new creative possibilities.

Highlight: The Pixel 9 Pro XL's camera empowers you to capture stunning photos with ease. By understanding the camera interface, shooting modes, and basic photography principles, you can unlock your creative potential and preserve life's precious moments in beautiful photographs.

Astrophotography Mode

The Google Pixel 9 Pro XL's camera isn't just limited to capturing the beauty of the Earth; it can also capture the wonders of the night sky. With Astrophotography mode, you can take stunning photos of stars, constellations, and even the Milky Way, all with the convenience of your smartphone.

Activating Astrophotography Mode

> ➤ Stable Setup: For the best results, you'll need a tripod or a stable surface to keep your Pixel 9 Pro XL perfectly still during the long exposure.

> ➤ Night Sight: Open the Camera app and switch to Night Sight mode.

> ➤ Detect the Stars: Point your Pixel at the night sky. The camera will automatically detect that you're trying to capture stars and will suggest switching to Astrophotography mode.

> ➤ Activate: Tap on the suggestion or manually select Astrophotography mode from the mode selector.

Capturing Stellar Shots

> • Focus: The camera will automatically focus on the stars. You can also manually adjust the focus by tapping on the screen.

> • Exposure: Astrophotography mode uses long exposures to capture more light from the stars. The exposure time will automatically adjust based on the darkness of the sky and the stability of your phone.

You can see the estimated capture time on the screen.

- Capture: Tap the shutter button and hold your phone steady while the camera captures the image. The capture process can take several seconds or even minutes, depending on the conditions.

Tips for Astrophotography Success

➤ Dark Skies: Find a location with minimal light pollution for the best results. The darker the sky, the more stars you'll be able to capture.

➤ Stable Tripod: A sturdy tripod is essential for keeping your phone perfectly still during the long exposure. Even slight movements can result in blurry photos.

➤ Patience: Astrophotography requires patience. Be prepared to wait for the camera to capture the image, and don't be discouraged if your first few attempts aren't perfect.

➤ Experiment: Try different locations, angles, and settings to see how they affect your astrophotography shots.

Potential Challenges

- Light Pollution: Light pollution from cities and towns can make it difficult to capture faint stars.
- Clouds: Clouds can obscure the stars and ruin your astrophotography attempts. Check the weather forecast before heading out.
- Stability: Even with a tripod, slight vibrations or wind can cause blurry photos. Try to find a sheltered location or use a heavier tripod for better stability.

Highlight: Astrophotography mode on the Pixel 9 Pro XL unlocks a whole new world of photographic possibilities. With a bit of practice and patience, you can capture breathtaking images of the night sky that will amaze your friends and family.

Motion Mode and Advanced Photography Features

The Google Pixel 9 Pro XL's camera is packed with advanced features that go beyond basic point-and-shoot photography. Motion Mode, Top Shot, and Super Res Zoom are just a few of the tools that empower you to capture dynamic action shots, creative effects, and stunning details.

Motion Mode:

Motion Mode brings your photos to life by capturing movement in creative ways.

Action Pan: This mode blurs the background while keeping your subject sharp, creating a sense of speed and motion.

- Select Action Pan: Open the Camera app and switch to Motion Mode. Select "Action Pan."
- Focus on Your Subject: Tap on the subject you want to keep in focus.
- Capture: Hold your phone steady and pan it along with the moving subject as you take the photo.

Long Exposure: This mode captures light trails and motion blur, creating artistic and surreal effects.

- Select Long Exposure: In Motion Mode, select "Long Exposure."
- Find a Scene with Motion: Look for scenes with moving elements, such as flowing water, moving cars, or crowds of people.
- Capture: Hold your phone steady and capture the scene. The camera will automatically adjust the exposure time to create the long exposure effect.

Top Shot:

Top Shot helps you capture the best shot, even if you miss the perfect timing.

- How it Works: When you take a photo with Top Shot enabled, the camera captures a series of frames before and after you press the shutter button.
- Select the Best Shot: After taking the photo, you can review the frames and choose the one you like best.
- Enable Top Shot: Top Shot is usually enabled by default in certain modes, but you can check its settings in the Camera app.

Super Res Zoom:

Super Res Zoom uses AI to enhance the detail and clarity of zoomed-in photos.

- How it Works: When you zoom in, the camera captures multiple frames and combines them to create a higher-resolution image.
- Use Super Res Zoom: Simply pinch in or out on the viewfinder to zoom in or out. The camera will automatically use Super Res Zoom when you zoom beyond the optical zoom range.

Tips for Advanced Photography

➢ Practice: Mastering these advanced features might require some practice. Experiment with different settings and scenarios to see how they affect your photos.

➢ Stability: For Motion Mode and Long Exposure, a stable hand or a tripod is crucial for sharp results.

➢ Creativity: Don't be afraid to get creative and try new things. These advanced features offer a wide range of creative possibilities.

Highlight: The Pixel 9 Pro XL's advanced photography features empower you to go beyond basic photography and capture stunning images with creative flair. Whether you're freezing action with Motion Mode, capturing the perfect moment with Top Shot, or zooming in on the details with Super Res Zoom, your Pixel unlocks a world of photographic potential.

Recording Videos

The Google Pixel 9 Pro XL's camera isn't just a still-image marvel; it's also a powerful video recording tool. Whether you're capturing family memories, documenting your adventures, or creating cinematic masterpieces, your Pixel offers a range of video recording modes and settings to help you capture stunning footage.

The Video Recording Interface
- ➤ Open Camera App: Open the Camera app on your Pixel 9 Pro XL.
- ➤ Switch to Video Mode: Swipe left or right on the mode selector to switch to Video mode.

Key Elements:
- ➤ Viewfinder: This shows the live preview of what you're recording.
- ➤ Record Button: Tap this button to start and stop recording.
- ➤ Zoom Controls: Pinch in or out on the viewfinder to zoom in or out.
- ➤ Settings: Tap the gear icon to access video recording settings, such as resolution, frame rate, and stabilization.

Video Recording Modes and Settings
Resolution and Frame Rate: The Pixel 9 Pro XL supports various video resolutions and frame rates, including:
- 4K: Record stunning 4K video at up to 60 frames per second (fps) for ultra-high definition footage.

- 1080p: Record in Full HD at various frame rates, including 30fps and 60fps.
- Slow Motion: Capture slow-motion videos at different frame rates, such as 120fps or 240fps, to highlight details and create dramatic effects.

Video Stabilization: Reduce camera shake and create smoother videos with video stabilization. You can usually choose between different stabilization modes, such as Standard and Cinematic.

Other Features: Explore other video recording features, such as:
- Timelapse: Capture a timelapse video to condense a long event into a short and captivating clip.
- Cinematic Blur: Add a shallow depth of field to your videos for a cinematic look.
- Live HDR+: Enhance the dynamic range of your videos for vibrant colors and balanced exposure.

Tips for Recording High-Quality Videos
- ➢ Lighting: Good lighting is crucial for video quality. Shoot in well-lit environments whenever possible.
- ➢ Stability: Avoid excessive camera movement to prevent shaky footage. Use a tripod or gimbal for

smoother videos, especially when using zoom or slow motion.

- ➢ Audio: Pay attention to the audio quality. Use an external microphone if needed, especially in noisy environments.
- ➢ Focus: Make sure your subject is in focus. Tap on the viewfinder to focus on a specific area.
- ➢ Composition: Think about the composition of your video. Use the rule of thirds and other composition techniques to create visually appealing shots.

Editing Photos and Videos

The Google Pixel 9 Pro XL doesn't just help you capture stunning photos and videos; it also provides powerful editing tools to refine your creations and add a personal touch. Whether you want to crop a photo, apply a filter, adjust colors, or add text, your Pixel has you covered.

Photo Editing

- ➢ Open Google Photos: Open the Google Photos app, where your photos and videos are stored.
- ➢ Select a Photo: Choose the photo you want to edit.
- ➢ Access Editing Tools: Tap on the Edit icon (usually a pencil icon) at the bottom of the screen.

Explore Editing Options: You'll find a variety of editing tools, including:

- Crop and Rotate: Crop your photo to focus on the subject or rotate it to adjust the orientation.
- Filters: Apply different filters to change the mood and style of your photo.
- Adjustments: Fine-tune brightness, contrast, shadows, highlights, and other aspects of your photo.
- Markup: Add text, drawings, and shapes to your photo.
- Magic Eraser: Remove unwanted objects from your photo with a tap.
- Photo Unblur: Sharpen blurry photos to restore clarity.

Save Your Edits: Once you're happy with your edits, tap "Save copy" to save a new version of the photo while preserving the original.

Video Editing

- ➢ Open Google Photos: Open the Google Photos app and select the video you want to edit.
- ➢ Access Editing Tools: Tap on the Edit icon at the bottom of the screen.

Explore Editing Options: You'll find video editing tools, including:

- Trim: Trim the beginning or end of your video to remove unwanted footage.
- Stabilize: Reduce camera shake and create smoother videos.
- Adjustments: Adjust brightness, contrast, and other aspects of your video.
- Filters: Apply different filters to change the mood and style of your video.
- Add Music: Add music from your library or Google's library to your video.

Save Your Edits: Tap "Save copy" to save a new version of the video with your edits.

Third-Party Editing Apps

> While the Pixel 9 Pro XL's built-in editing tools are powerful, you might prefer using third-party editing apps for more advanced features and creative control. Explore the Google Play Store for apps like Adobe Lightroom, Snapseed, and FilmoraGo to expand your editing possibilities.

Highlight: The Pixel 9 Pro XL empowers you to not only capture stunning photos and videos but also transform them into polished masterpieces. With its intuitive editing tools and AI-powered features, you can unleash your creativity and personalize your visual content with ease.

Managing Camera Settings

The Google Pixel 9 Pro XL's camera offers a wealth of settings that allow you to fine-tune your photography experience and capture images exactly as you envision them. Whether you want to adjust resolution, change aspect ratios, enable gridlines, or explore other advanced options, this guide will help you navigate the camera settings and unlock the full potential of your Pixel's camera.

Accessing Camera Settings

> ➤ Open Camera App: Open the Camera app on your Pixel 9 Pro XL.
> ➤ Tap the Gear Icon: In the camera interface, tap the gear icon (usually located in the top-left or top-right corner) to access the camera settings menu.

Key Camera Settings

Resolution and Aspect Ratio:

- Resolution: Choose the resolution of your photos and videos. Higher resolutions capture more detail but result in larger file sizes.

- Aspect Ratio: Select the aspect ratio of your photos, such as 4:3, 16:9, or 1:1 (square).

Gridlines:

- Enable Gridlines: Overlay gridlines on the viewfinder to help you compose your shots using the rule of thirds or other composition techniques.

Timer:

- Set Timer Delay: Set a timer to delay the shutter release, giving you time to get in the shot or set up the perfect composition.

HDR+:

- Adjust HDR+ Intensity: HDR+ (High Dynamic Range) captures multiple exposures and combines them to create a photo with balanced highlights and shadows. You can adjust its intensity or turn it off completely.

Flash:

- Control the Flash: Choose between Auto, On, and Off modes for the flash.

Video Stabilization:

- Select Stabilization Mode: Choose between different video stabilization modes, such as Standard and Cinematic.

Storage Location:

- Choose Storage: Select whether to save photos and videos to your phone's internal storage or a microSD card (if inserted).

Other Settings: Explore other camera settings, such as:

- ➤ Google Lens: Use Google Lens to identify objects, translate text, and search for information about what you see through the camera.
- ➤ Level: Display a level indicator to help you keep your shots straight.
- ➤ Location: Tag your photos and videos with location information.

Tips for Managing Camera Settings

- Don't be afraid to experiment with different camera settings to see how they affect your photos and videos.
- Reset to Default: If you're not happy with your changes, you can always reset the camera settings to their default values.
- Read the Tooltips: Many camera settings have tooltips that provide brief explanations of their functions. Tap and hold on a setting to see its tooltip.

APPS AND SOFTWARE

Exploring Pre-installed Apps

The Google Pixel 9 Pro XL comes equipped with a suite of pre-installed apps designed to enhance your productivity, entertainment, and overall mobile experience. These apps seamlessly integrate with Google's ecosystem, offering a cohesive and user-friendly environment. Let's explore some of the key pre-installed apps and their functionalities.

Essential Google Apps

- ➤ Gmail: Google's email service, allowing you to send, receive, and manage your emails with ease.
- ➤ Google Maps: Navigate the world with detailed maps, real-time traffic updates, and turn-by-turn navigation.
- ➤ Google Photos: Store, organize, and share your photos and videos. Enjoy unlimited storage for photos and videos backed up in "Storage Saver" quality.
- ➤ Google Drive: Store and access your files in the cloud, including documents, spreadsheets, and presentations.

➢ Google Chrome: Browse the web with Google's fast and secure web browser.

➢ YouTube: Watch and discover videos from around the world, including music videos, educational content, and entertainment.

➢ Google Play Store: Download and install apps, games, movies, music, and books from Google's vast digital content library.

➢ Google Calendar: Manage your schedule, set reminders, and share events with others.

➢ Google Keep: Capture notes, lists, and photos to keep track of your ideas and tasks.

➢ Google Meet: Connect with others through video calls and conferences.

Other Useful Apps

- Calculator: Perform basic and scientific calculations.
- Clock: Set alarms, timers, and view the time in different time zones.
- Contacts: Store and manage your contacts.
- Files: Manage files stored on your phone and in the cloud.
- Phone: Make and receive phone calls.
- Messages: Send and receive text messages (SMS) and multimedia messages (MMS).

- Recorder: Record audio notes and conversations.

The Power of Google's Ecosystem

The pre-installed Google apps on your Pixel 9 Pro XL work together seamlessly, creating a unified and efficient experience. For example:

- Share Photos Easily: Share photos directly from Google Photos to other Google apps like Gmail or Messages.
- Seamless Navigation: Get directions in Google Maps and easily share them with friends through other apps.
- Integrated Calendar: Events and reminders created in Google Calendar can be accessed and managed from other Google apps.

Highlight: The Pixel 9 Pro XL's pre-installed apps provide a comprehensive toolkit for productivity, communication, and entertainment. The tight integration with Google's ecosystem enhances the user experience and simplifies everyday tasks. Take some time to explore these apps and discover how they can streamline your digital life.

Downloading and Installing Apps from Google Play

The Google Play Store is your gateway to a vast world of apps, games, movies, music, and books, ready to enhance your Pixel 9 Pro XL experience. With millions of apps to choose from, you can customize your phone to fit your interests and needs. Let's explore how to navigate the Play Store and install new apps on your Pixel.

Navigating the Google Play Store

➢ Open the Play Store: Tap on the Play Store icon on your home screen or in the app drawer.

➢ Explore Categories: Browse through different categories, such as "Games," "Apps," "Movies & TV," and "Books," to discover new content.

➢ Search for Apps: Use the search bar at the top of the screen to find specific apps by name or keyword.

➢ App Pages: When you find an app you're interested in, tap on it to view its details, including screenshots, descriptions, reviews, and ratings.

Installing Apps

➢ Tap "Install": On the app's page, tap the green "Install" button.

➢ Grant Permissions: You might be asked to grant certain permissions to the app, such as access to your location, contacts, or camera. Review the permissions carefully before granting them.

➢ Download and Installation: The app will start downloading and installing on your phone. You can see the progress in the notification shade.

➢ Open the App: Once the installation is complete, you can open the app by tapping the "Open" button in the Play Store or by tapping on its icon on your home screen or in the app drawer.

Troubleshooting Tips

- Google Account Issues: If you're having trouble downloading or installing apps, make sure you're signed in to your Google account and that your account is in good standing. You can check your account status by going to Settings > Accounts > Google.

- Finding Specific Apps: If you're having trouble finding a specific app, try using different keywords or browsing through relevant categories. You can also check the app's official website for a direct link to its Play Store page.

- Storage Space: Make sure you have enough storage space on your phone to install the app. You can check your storage space by going to Settings > Storage.

Highlight: The Google Play Store offers a vast and diverse selection of apps, allowing you to personalize your Pixel 9 Pro XL and unlock its full potential. Whether you're looking for productivity tools, entertainment apps, or creative outlets, the Play Store has something for everyone.

Managing Installed Applications

Your Google Pixel 9 Pro XL allows you to take control of your app ecosystem, ensuring you have the apps you need, keeping them updated, and managing their permissions to protect your privacy. Whether you want to uninstall unwanted apps, update to the latest versions, or fine-tune app permissions, this guide will walk you through the process.

Uninstalling Apps
- Locate the App: Find the app you want to uninstall on your home screen or in the app drawer.

Uninstall Options:

- From Home Screen: Touch and hold the app icon, and then select "Uninstall."
- From App Drawer: Open the app drawer, touch and hold the app icon, and drag it to the "Uninstall" option at the top of the screen.
- From Settings: Go to Settings > Apps > See all apps, select the app, and tap "Uninstall."

Confirm Uninstall: A pop-up will ask you to confirm the uninstallation. Tap "OK" to proceed.

Caution: Be careful not to uninstall important system apps or apps that you might need later.

Updating Apps

Keeping your apps updated ensures you have the latest features, bug fixes, and security enhancements.

- ➤ Open Play Store: Open the Google Play Store app.
- ➤ Manage Apps & Device: Tap on your profile picture in the top right corner and select "Manage apps & device."

Update Apps:

- Update All: Tap "Update all" to update all apps with available updates.

- Selective Updates: Tap "See details" to view available updates for individual apps. Select the apps you want to update and tap "Update."

Managing App Permissions

App permissions control what data and features an app can access on your phone. It's important to review and manage app permissions to protect your privacy and security.

- Go to App Info: Go to Settings > Apps > See all apps and select the app you want to manage.
- App Permissions: Tap on "Permissions" to see a list of permissions the app has requested.
- Modify Permissions: You can grant or revoke permissions for the app. Consider carefully whether the app truly needs the requested permissions.

Important Notes:

➤ Essential Permissions: Some apps require certain permissions to function properly. Revoking essential permissions might cause the app to malfunction.
➤ Permission Categories: Permissions are categorized based on their sensitivity, such as location, camera, contacts, and storage.

Highlight: Managing your installed applications is crucial for maintaining a healthy and secure app ecosystem on your Pixel 9 Pro XL. By uninstalling unwanted apps, keeping apps updated, and carefully managing app permissions, you can optimize your phone's performance, protect your privacy, and enjoy a smooth and personalized mobile experience.

Google Tensor Chip and AI Enhancements

The Google Pixel 9 Pro XL is powered by the revolutionary Google Tensor G5 processor, a chip designed specifically for Pixel devices to deliver a unique and enhanced user experience. This isn't just about raw speed; Tensor G5 brings together cutting-edge AI and machine learning capabilities to make your phone smarter, faster, and more intuitive than ever before.

What is Google Tensor?

Google Tensor is a system on a chip (SoC) that combines multiple components, including the CPU, GPU, and TPU (Tensor Processing Unit), into a single integrated circuit. This integrated design allows for optimized performance and power efficiency.

- CPU: The central processing unit handles the core tasks and operations of your phone.
- GPU: The graphics processing unit renders images and videos, providing smooth visuals and gaming experiences.
- TPU: The Tensor Processing Unit is specifically designed for AI and machine learning tasks, enabling features like real-time language translation, image recognition, and voice assistance.

The Tensor Advantage

- Enhanced Performance: The Tensor G5 chip delivers exceptional performance across all tasks, from launching apps to playing graphics-intensive games. You'll experience smooth multitasking, faster processing speeds, and overall responsiveness.
- AI-Powered Features: Tensor G5 unlocks a new level of AI capabilities on your Pixel 9 Pro XL. This translates to features like:
- Live Translate: Translate conversations in real-time, breaking down language barriers.
- Magic Eraser: Remove unwanted objects from photos with a tap.
- Photo Unblur: Sharpen blurry photos, even old ones from your library.

- Call Screen: Google Assistant answers calls for you and filters out spam.
- Hold for Me: Google Assistant waits on hold for you during calls, so you don't have to.
- Power Efficiency: The integrated design of the Tensor G5 chip optimizes power consumption, leading to longer battery life for your Pixel 9 Pro XL.

The Subtle Power of AI

While the impact of the Tensor G5 chip might not always be immediately obvious, it works behind the scenes to enhance your everyday experience in subtle but significant ways:

- Faster App Launches: Apps launch quicker and run smoother thanks to the optimized performance of the Tensor G5 chip.
- Improved Camera Performance: The camera benefits from the Tensor G5's AI processing, resulting in faster image processing, better low-light performance, and more accurate scene recognition.
- Personalized Experiences: The AI capabilities of the Tensor G5 chip enable personalized experiences, such as customized recommendations, smarter notifications, and more intuitive interactions with your phone.

Highlight: The Google Tensor G5 chip is more than just a processor; it's the brain that powers the Pixel 9 Pro XL's intelligence and performance. With its advanced AI capabilities and optimized design, Tensor G5 delivers a unique and enhanced mobile experience that sets the Pixel apart from the crowd.

Live Translation

Imagine having a conversation with someone who speaks a different language, and understanding each other effortlessly. With Live Translate on your Google Pixel 9 Pro XL, this is no longer a fantasy. Powered by the Google Tensor G5 processor, Live Translate breaks down language barriers and opens up a world of communication possibilities.

Activating Live Translate

Live Translate is seamlessly integrated into various apps and features on your Pixel 9 Pro XL. Here are a few ways to access it:

➢ During a Conversation: When you're in a conversation with someone who speaks a different language, Live Translate can automatically detect the languages being spoken and provide real-time translations. You'll see the translated text on your screen, allowing you to follow along and respond accordingly.

➢ In Messaging Apps: Live Translate can also translate text within messaging apps like Google Messages and WhatsApp. Simply select the text you want to translate, and the translation will appear instantly.

➢ Using the Camera: Point your camera at text in a foreign language, such as signs, menus, or documents, and Live Translate will overlay the translated text on the screen in real-time.

Using Live Translate

- Language Selection: Make sure the languages you want to translate are selected in the Live Translate settings. You can access these settings by going to Settings > System > Live Translate.

- Activate Live Translate: Depending on the scenario, Live Translate might activate automatically, or you might need to tap a button or icon to initiate the translation.

- Speak or Type: Speak naturally or type your message, and Live Translate will provide real-time translations.

- View Translations: The translated text will appear on your screen, allowing you to understand the conversation or read the text in your preferred language.

Potential Challenges

➤ Accuracy: While Live Translate is generally accurate, it might encounter challenges with certain languages or dialects, especially those with complex grammatical structures or limited training data.

➤ Noisy Environments: Background noise can interfere with speech recognition, potentially affecting the accuracy of Live Translate.

➤ Internet Connection: Live Translate requires an internet connection to function.

Tips for Optimal Performance

- Speak Clearly: Speak clearly and at a moderate pace to improve speech recognition accuracy.

- Reduce Background Noise: Try to use Live Translate in quiet environments to minimize interference.

- Check Internet Connection: Ensure you have a stable internet connection for seamless translation.

Highlight: Live Translate on the Pixel 9 Pro XL is a game-changer for communication, breaking down language barriers and fostering understanding between people from different cultures. Whether you're traveling abroad, communicating with international colleagues, or simply trying to understand a foreign language menu, Live Translate empowers you to connect with the world around you.

Call Screening

Tired of unwanted calls disrupting your day? The Google Pixel 9 Pro XL offers a powerful feature called Call Screening that helps you filter out spam and robocalls, giving you peace of mind and control over your phone calls.

Enabling Call Screening

➢ Open Phone App: Open the Phone app on your Pixel 9 Pro XL.

➢ Access Call Screen Settings: Tap the three dots in the top right corner of the Phone app to access the call settings menu. Then, select "Spam and Call Screen."

Enable Call Screen: Choose how you want Call Screen to handle calls:

- See the caller and spam ID: This option displays caller ID information and identifies potential spam calls, allowing you to decide whether to answer or decline.
- Filter spam calls: Automatically screens suspected spam calls and sends them to voicemail.
- Silence unknown callers: Silences calls from numbers that aren't in your contacts.

Using Call Screen

When a call comes in that's being screened, you'll see the "Call Screen" interface:

➢ See Caller Information: The screen displays information about the caller, including their phone number and any available caller ID details.

➢ Google Assistant Answers: Google Assistant answers the call on your behalf and asks the caller to identify themselves and the reason for their call.

➢ View Transcript: You can see a real-time transcript of the conversation between Google Assistant and the caller.

Choose an Action: Based on the transcript, you can choose to:

- Answer: Answer the call if it seems legitimate.
- Decline: Decline the call and send it to voicemail.

- Report as Spam: Report the call as spam to help improve future call screening accuracy.

Potential Challenges
- ➤ Missed Important Calls: If Call Screening is set to automatically filter or silence calls, you might miss important calls from unknown numbers, such as calls from delivery services or healthcare providers.
- ➤ False Positives: Call Screening might occasionally misidentify legitimate calls as spam.

Tips for Effective Call Screening
- Customize Settings: Adjust the Call Screen settings to find the right balance between filtering unwanted calls and ensuring you don't miss important calls.
- Review Call History: Regularly review your call history and screened calls to identify any potential false positives or missed important calls.
- Add Important Numbers to Contacts: Add phone numbers for important contacts, such as doctors, delivery services, and schools, to your contact list to prevent them from being screened.

Highlight: Call Screening on the Pixel 9 Pro XL is a powerful tool for taking control of your calls and reducing unwanted interruptions. By utilizing Google Assistant's intelligence and customizable settings, you can effectively filter out spam calls and enjoy peace of mind.

AI-driven Features (Suggestions and Personalization)

The Google Pixel 9 Pro XL leverages the power of artificial intelligence (AI) to provide a personalized and intuitive user experience. From suggesting smart replies to optimizing battery life and recommending relevant apps, AI is seamlessly integrated into various aspects of your Pixel, making it a truly intelligent companion.

Smart Compose:

Smart Compose uses AI to predict your next words as you type, offering suggestions for completing sentences and phrases in messaging apps like Google Messages and Gmail. This feature saves you time and effort, making communication faster and more efficient.

- How it Works: Smart Compose analyzes your writing style and context to provide relevant suggestions. It learns from your previous conversations and adapts to your preferences over time.

- Accept Suggestions: To accept a suggestion, simply swipe right on the suggested word or phrase.

Adaptive Battery:

Adaptive Battery uses AI to learn your app usage patterns and optimize battery consumption. It prioritizes battery power for the apps you use most frequently, while limiting battery usage for less important apps.

- How it Works: Adaptive Battery identifies apps that you rarely use and puts them in a "restricted" state, preventing them from running in the background and consuming unnecessary power.
- Enable Adaptive Battery: Go to Settings > Battery > Adaptive Battery and toggle it on.

Personalized App Recommendations

The Pixel 9 Pro XL uses AI to provide personalized app recommendations based on your usage patterns and interests. You'll see these recommendations in the Play Store and other app discovery platforms.

- How it Works: AI analyzes your app usage history, the types of apps you typically download, and your interests to suggest relevant apps that you might enjoy.

- Discover New Apps: Explore the "Recommended for you" section in the Play Store to find new apps tailored to your preferences.

Other AI-Powered Features

➢ Call Screen: Google Assistant answers calls for you and filters out spam.

➢ Hold for Me: Google Assistant waits on hold for you during calls, so you don't have to.

➢ Live Caption: Automatically generate captions for audio playing on your phone.

➢ Now Playing: Identify songs playing in your environment without having to search for them.

➢ Google Assistant: Get personalized assistance, answers to your questions, and help with everyday tasks.

Addressing Privacy Concerns

Google is committed to protecting your privacy. The AI features on your Pixel 9 Pro XL are designed to process data in a privacy-preserving manner.

- On-device Processing: Many AI features, like Smart Compose and Now Playing, process data directly on your device, minimizing the need to send data to Google's servers.
- Data Minimization: Google collects only the necessary data to provide and improve AI features.
- User Control: You have control over your privacy settings and can choose which data is used for personalization.

Highlight: The Pixel 9 Pro XL's AI-driven features provide a personalized and intuitive mobile experience. By leveraging the power of AI, your Pixel can anticipate your needs, optimize performance, and offer helpful suggestions, making it a truly intelligent companion. Google's commitment to privacy ensures that your data is handled responsibly and that you have control over your personalization settings.

Android 14 Features

The Google Pixel 9 Pro XL comes with the latest and greatest version of Android: Android 14. This new iteration of Android brings a fresh look, enhanced privacy features, performance optimizations, and a host of other improvements to elevate your mobile experience.

Visual Refresh

Android 14 introduces subtle but noticeable visual changes to the user interface, creating a more modern and refined aesthetic.

- Updated Icons and Colors: System icons and colors have been refreshed for a more consistent and visually appealing look.
- Refined Animations: Animations and transitions have been refined for a smoother and more fluid user experience.
- Improved Typography: The system font has been updated for better readability and clarity.

Privacy at the Forefront

Android 14 doubles down on privacy with enhanced controls and features to protect your data.

- More Granular App Permissions: Gain finer control over app permissions, allowing you to grant or deny access to specific data types, such as location, camera, and microphone, on a per-app basis.
- Improved Privacy Dashboard: The Privacy Dashboard provides a clearer overview of how apps

are accessing your data, making it easier to identify and manage potential privacy risks.

- Enhanced Location Controls: Choose to share your precise location or only your approximate location with apps.

Performance Boost

Android 14 includes under-the-hood optimizations to improve performance and battery life.

- Faster App Launches: Apps launch quicker and run smoother thanks to improved memory management and background process optimization.
- Extended Battery Life: Enjoy longer battery life with optimizations that reduce power consumption for background processes and idle apps.
- Smoother Performance: Experience a more fluid and responsive user interface with optimized animations and transitions.

Other Notable Features

➢ Enhanced Accessibility: Android 14 includes new accessibility features and improvements, such as improved screen reader support and more customizable accessibility settings.

➤ Improved Sharing: Share content more easily with improved sharing options and a redesigned share sheet.

➤ Updated Notifications: Notifications have been refined for better organization and clarity.

➤ New Lock Screen Customization: Personalize your lock screen with new clock styles, widgets, and shortcuts.

Adapting to the Changes

While most of the changes in Android 14 are designed to be intuitive, some users might need time to adjust to the new features and interface elements.

- Explore the Settings: Take some time to explore the Settings app and familiarize yourself with the new options and controls.

- Use Tutorials: Android 14 might include tutorials and tips to guide you through the new features.

Highlight: Android 14 on your Pixel 9 Pro XL delivers a fresh, refined, and secure mobile experience. With its visual refresh, enhanced privacy controls, performance optimizations, and other improvements, Android 14 elevates your Pixel to a new level of sophistication and usability.

SECURITY AND DATA BACKUP

Setting Up Screen Lock and Biometrics

Your Google Pixel 9 Pro XL holds a treasure trove of personal information, from private messages and photos to financial details and sensitive documents. Protecting this data is paramount, and your Pixel offers robust security features, including various screen lock options and convenient biometric authentication.

Setting Up a Screen Lock
Access Security Settings: Go to Settings > Security.
Choose Screen Lock: Tap on "Screen lock" to explore the available options:

- ➤ PIN: A numerical code that you enter to unlock your phone.
- ➤ Password: A combination of letters, numbers, and symbols for stronger security.
- ➤ Pattern: A pattern that you draw on the screen to unlock your phone.
- ➤ Fingerprint: Use your unique fingerprint to unlock your phone quickly and securely.

➤ Face Recognition: Unlock your phone with a glance using the front-facing camera.

Follow the Prompts: Follow the on-screen instructions to set up your chosen screen lock method. You'll typically be asked to enter your PIN, password, or pattern twice to confirm it.

Enrolling Biometrics

Biometric authentication provides a convenient and secure way to unlock your phone using your unique physical characteristics.

Fingerprint:

Go to Biometric Settings: Go to Settings > Security > Fingerprint Unlock.

Enroll Fingerprint: Follow the on-screen instructions to place your finger on the fingerprint sensor multiple times to register your fingerprint.

Face Recognition:

Go to Biometric Settings: Go to Settings > Security > Face Unlock.

Enroll Face: Follow the on-screen prompts to position your face within the frame and scan your facial features.

Important Notes

- Strong Passwords: Choose strong and unique passwords or patterns that are difficult for others to guess.
- Biometric Security: While convenient, biometrics might not be as secure as strong passwords or PINs. Keep this in mind when choosing your screen lock method.
- Forgot Screen Lock: If you forget your screen lock, you might need to factory reset your phone, which will erase all your data. Be sure to remember your screen lock or set up a backup method.

Highlight: Securing your Pixel 9 Pro XL is essential for protecting your personal information. By utilizing a strong screen lock and convenient biometric authentication, you can strike a balance between security and ease of access. Remember, your phone is a valuable tool, and taking the necessary steps to secure it ensures your digital world remains private and protected.

Find My Device

Losing your phone can be a stressful experience. Thankfully, the Google Pixel 9 Pro XL comes with Find My Device, a powerful tool that helps you locate your phone if it's lost or stolen. It also allows you to remotely lock your phone or erase its data to protect your personal information.

Enabling Find My Device

Find My Device is usually enabled by default, but it's always a good idea to double-check:

> ➤ Go to Settings: Open the Settings app on your Pixel 9 Pro XL.
> ➤ Find My Device: Go to Security > Find My Device.
> ➤ Ensure it's On: Make sure the toggle is turned on.

Using Find My Device

If you lose your phone, you can use Find My Device to locate it from another device, such as a computer or another phone.

Access Find My Device:

- Website: Go to android.com/find on a computer or another phone.
- App: Download the "Find My Device" app from the Google Play Store on another Android device.
- Sign In: Sign in with the same Google account that's signed in on your lost Pixel 9 Pro XL.

Locate Your Phone: Find My Device will show you the last known location of your phone on a map. If your phone is online and location services are enabled, you'll see its current location.

Take Action: You can take several actions remotely:
- ➤ Play Sound: Make your phone ring at full volume, even if it's on silent, to help you locate it if it's nearby.
- ➤ Secure Device: Lock your phone with a password and display a message on the lock screen, such as your contact information.
- ➤ Erase Device: Erase all data on your phone to protect your personal information. This is a last resort option, as it will permanently delete everything on your phone.

Potential Challenges
- Phone is Off or Offline: Find My Device relies on your phone being turned on and connected to the internet to provide its location and enable remote actions. If your phone is turned off or has no internet connection, Find My Device might not be able to locate it or perform actions.

- Location Accuracy: The accuracy of the location information provided by Find My Device depends on various factors, such as GPS signal strength and availability.

Highlight: Find My Device is an essential tool for any Pixel 9 Pro XL owner. By enabling this feature and understanding how to use it, you can increase your chances of recovering your lost phone or protecting your data if it falls into the wrong hands. Remember, prevention is key, so take the time to set up Find My Device today.

Security Updates and Google Play Protect

Your Google Pixel 9 Pro XL is designed with security in mind, but staying protected from evolving threats requires staying up-to-date with the latest security patches and utilizing built-in security features like Google Play Protect.

Security Updates:
Security updates are like regular check-ups for your phone's immune system. They contain patches that address vulnerabilities and protect against malware, viruses, and other security threats.

Why They Matter: Cybersecurity threats are constantly evolving. New vulnerabilities are discovered regularly, and hackers are always looking for ways to exploit them. Security updates close these loopholes, keeping your phone and your data safe.

Pixel's Advantage: Pixel phones receive regular security updates directly from Google, ensuring you have the latest protection.

Installing Updates:
- Check for Updates: Go to Settings > System > System update.
- Download and Install: If an update is available, tap "Download and install." It's best to connect to Wi-Fi before downloading updates to avoid using mobile data.
- Restart: Your phone will restart to apply the update.

Google Play Protect:
Google Play Protect is a built-in security feature that automatically scans apps on your Pixel 9 Pro XL for malware and other harmful software.

➤ Real-time Protection: Play Protect continuously scans apps on your phone, even those installed from sources other than the Play Store.

➤ Harmful App Detection: If Play Protect detects a harmful app, it will notify you and might take action to protect your phone, such as disabling the app or prompting you to uninstall it.

➤ Safe Browsing: Play Protect also helps protect you from harmful websites when you're browsing the web with Chrome.

➤ Verify Apps: You can manually scan apps for harmful behavior by going to Play Store > (Your Profile Icon) > Play Protect > Scan.

Potential Challenges

• Delayed Updates: Some users might delay installing security updates due to inconvenience or concerns about potential bugs. However, delaying updates leaves your phone vulnerable to security threats.

• Disabled Play Protect: Some users might accidentally or intentionally disable Google Play Protect, leaving their phone exposed to potentially harmful apps.

Highlight: Keeping your Pixel 9 Pro XL updated with the latest security patches and utilizing Google Play Protect are crucial steps in safeguarding your phone and your data. By prioritizing security, you can enjoy a worry-free mobile experience knowing that your Pixel is protected from evolving threats.

Data Permissions and Management

Your Google Pixel 9 Pro XL gives you control over your data and how apps access it. Understanding and managing app permissions is crucial for protecting your privacy and ensuring that apps only access the information they truly need to function.

App Permissions:

App permissions determine what data and features an app can access on your phone. You can grant or deny these permissions on a per-app basis.

> ➤ Access App Info: Go to Settings > Apps > See all apps and select the app you want to manage.
> ➤ Permissions: Tap on "Permissions" to see a list of permissions the app has requested or been granted.

Modify Permissions:

- Allowed: Permissions that the app is currently allowed to access.
- Denied: Permissions that the app is not allowed to access.

Tap on a permission category (e.g., Location, Camera, Contacts) to modify its settings. You can choose to:

- Allow all the time: The app can access this data even when you're not using it.
- Allow only while using the app: The app can access this data only when it's actively open and in use.
- Ask every time: The app will ask for your permission each time it needs to access this data.
- Don't allow: The app is completely blocked from accessing this data.

Understanding Permission Categories

Permissions are categorized based on their sensitivity and potential impact on your privacy:

- Location: Allows the app to access your phone's location.
- Camera: Allows the app to use your phone's camera to take photos or videos.
- Microphone: Allows the app to record audio.
- Contacts: Allows the app to access your contacts list.

- Storage: Allows the app to access files stored on your phone.
- Phone: Allows the app to make and manage phone calls.
- SMS: Allows the app to send and receive text messages.
- Calendar: Allows the app to access your calendar events.
- Sensors: Allows the app to access data from your phone's sensors, such as the accelerometer and gyroscope.

Managing Data Usage

You can also control how much data individual apps are allowed to use, especially when you're on a limited mobile data plan.

- ➢ Go to Data Usage: Go to Settings > Network & internet > Internet > App data usage.
- ➢ Select an App: Tap on the app you want to manage.
- ➢ Restrict Background Data: Toggle on "Restrict background data" to prevent the app from using data when it's not actively in use.

Tips for Data Privacy

> ➤ Review Permissions Carefully: Before granting permissions to an app, consider whether the app truly needs that access to function properly.

> ➤ Minimize Permissions: Grant only the necessary permissions to apps. You can always grant additional permissions later if needed.

> ➤ Regularly Review App Permissions: Periodically review the permissions you've granted to apps and revoke any unnecessary permissions.

> ➤ Stay Informed: Stay informed about app privacy policies and best practices for data protection.

Highlight: Taking control of your data and app permissions is crucial for protecting your privacy on your Pixel 9 Pro XL. By understanding how to manage app permissions and data usage, you can ensure that your personal information remains secure and that apps only access the data they need to provide their services.

Backup and Restore Data

Our phones have become repositories of precious memories, important documents, and essential data. Losing this information can be devastating. Thankfully, the Google

Pixel 9 Pro XL offers easy and reliable ways to back up and restore your data, ensuring that your valuable information is always safe and accessible.

Backing Up Your Data

Backing up your data creates a copy of your phone's information, including apps, contacts, photos, videos, settings, and more, and stores it securely in the cloud or on another device.

1. Back Up to Google Drive:
- Enable Backup: Go to Settings > System > Backup. Make sure "Back up to Google Drive" is turned on.
- Choose What to Back Up: Select the types of data you want to back up, such as app data, call history, contacts, device settings, and photos & videos.
- Initiate Backup: Tap "Back up now" to start the backup process. You can also set up automatic backups to occur regularly.

2. Other Backup Options:
- Cloud Storage Services: Consider using other cloud storage services like Dropbox, OneDrive, or Box to back up specific files or folders.

- Computer: Connect your Pixel 9 Pro XL to your computer via USB and manually transfer important files to your computer's storage.

Restoring Your Data

You might need to restore your data in several scenarios, such as when you get a new phone, after a factory reset, or if you accidentally delete important data.

1. Restoring from Google Drive:
- Set Up New Phone: When you set up a new Pixel phone or after a factory reset, you'll be prompted to restore your data from a Google Drive backup.
- Select Backup: Choose the backup you want to restore from.
- Restore Data: Follow the on-screen prompts to restore your data.

2. Restoring from Other Sources:
- Cloud Storage: If you've backed up data to other cloud storage services, you can download and restore the data from those services.
- Computer: Connect your Pixel 9 Pro XL to your computer and manually transfer the backed-up files from your computer to your phone.

Potential Challenges

- ➤ Forgetting to Back Up: One of the biggest challenges is simply forgetting to back up your data regularly. Make it a habit to back up your phone periodically or enable automatic backups.
- ➤ Storage Space: Ensure you have enough storage space in Google Drive or other cloud services to accommodate your backups.
- ➤ Backup Errors: Occasionally, backup errors might occur. Check your backup settings and internet connection to troubleshoot any issues.

Highlight: Regularly backing up your Pixel 9 Pro XL's data is crucial for safeguarding your valuable information. By utilizing Google Drive or other backup methods, you can ensure that your memories, documents, and settings are always safe and accessible, even if you lose your phone or need to perform a factory reset.

BATTERY MANAGEMENT

Understanding Battery Usage

The Google Pixel 9 Pro XL is designed to provide long-lasting battery life, but understanding how your phone uses power can help you optimize battery consumption and extend the time between charges. Let's explore how to check battery usage statistics and identify power-hungry apps.

Checking Battery Usage

Open Battery Settings: Go to Settings > Battery.

Battery Usage Stats: You'll see an overview of your battery usage since the last full charge. This includes:

- Battery Level: The current battery percentage.
- Estimated Time Remaining: An estimate of how much longer your battery will last based on your current usage patterns.
- Battery Usage Graph: A visual representation of your battery level over time.

Identify Power-Hungry Apps: Scroll down to see a list of apps and their battery consumption percentages. This helps you identify apps that are using a significant amount of power.

Understanding Battery Usage Statistics

- ➤ App Usage: The percentage of battery used by each app.
- ➤ Background Activity: Some apps consume power even when they're not actively in use. This is referred to as background activity.
- ➤ System Processes: Essential system processes, such as the operating system and network connectivity, also consume battery power.

Tips for Reducing Battery Consumption

- Dim the Screen: Reduce screen brightness or enable adaptive brightness to automatically adjust brightness based on ambient lighting.
- Limit Background Activity: Restrict background activity for apps you don't use frequently. Go to Settings > Apps > See all apps, select the app, and toggle on "Restrict background data."
- Turn Off Unused Features: Disable features like Bluetooth, Wi-Fi, and location services when you're not using them.
- Use Dark Mode: On phones with OLED displays like the Pixel 9 Pro XL, using dark mode can save battery life because black pixels are essentially turned off.

- Optimize App Settings: Some apps have settings that can affect battery life. For example, you can reduce the refresh rate in some games or disable auto-play for videos in social media apps.
- Update Apps: Keep your apps updated. App updates often include performance improvements and bug fixes that can optimize battery usage.
- Extreme Battery Saver: When your battery is running low, enable Extreme Battery Saver mode to significantly extend battery life. This mode limits background activity and some app functionality.

Highlight: Understanding battery usage on your Pixel 9 Pro XL empowers you to take control of your power consumption and extend battery life. By identifying power-hungry apps and utilizing battery optimization techniques, you can ensure your Pixel is always ready when you need it.

5G Power Management Tips

5G connectivity on your Google Pixel 9 Pro XL unlocks blazing-fast speeds and enhanced experiences, but it can also consume more power than previous generations of mobile networks. To ensure you enjoy the benefits of 5G without sacrificing battery life, consider these power management tips:

Understanding 5G's Impact on Battery

➤ Higher Frequencies: 5G often utilizes higher frequencies that require more power to transmit and receive data.

➤ Increased Data Consumption: Faster speeds can lead to increased data consumption, which in turn puts a higher demand on the battery.

➤ Network Searching: Your phone might constantly search for 5G signals, even in areas with weak or no coverage, consuming additional power.

Tips for Optimizing 5G Power Consumption

● Monitor 5G Usage: Pay attention to how 5G usage affects your battery life. If you notice significant battery drain, consider adjusting your 5G settings or usage patterns.

● Switch to 4G When Possible: If you're in an area with weak or no 5G coverage, or if you don't require the high speeds of 5G, manually switch to 4G/LTE to conserve battery. You can do this in Settings > Network & internet > Mobile network > Preferred network type.

- Limit 5G for Data-Intensive Tasks: Reserve 5G for data-intensive tasks like downloading large files, streaming high-quality videos, or playing online games. For less demanding tasks like browsing the web or checking email, 4G might suffice.

- Optimize App Settings: Some apps have settings that can affect 5G data usage. For example, you can reduce the streaming quality for video apps or disable automatic downloads for social media apps.

- Use Wi-Fi When Available: Connect to Wi-Fi networks whenever possible to offload data traffic from 5G and conserve battery.

- Enable Data Saver: Turn on Data Saver mode in Settings > Network & internet > Internet > Data Saver to restrict background data usage and reduce overall data consumption, which can help conserve battery when using 5G.

- Keep Your Phone Cool: High temperatures can affect battery performance. Avoid using your phone in direct sunlight or excessively hot environments.

- Update Software: Make sure your Pixel 9 Pro XL's software is up to date. Software updates often include optimizations that can improve battery life, including 5G power management.

Highlight: Enjoying the benefits of 5G doesn't have to come at the expense of battery life. By understanding how 5G affects power consumption and utilizing these power management tips, you can strike a balance between speed and stamina, ensuring your Pixel 9 Pro XL is always ready for action.

Charging Your Device

The Google Pixel 9 Pro XL offers fast and convenient charging options to keep you powered up throughout your day. Whether you prefer the traditional wired method or the convenience of wireless charging, your Pixel has you covered.

Wired Charging
- USB-C: The Pixel 9 Pro XL uses a USB-C port for wired charging. This is the industry standard for modern smartphones, offering faster charging speeds and greater versatility compared to older micro-USB ports.
- Fast Charging: Your Pixel supports fast charging with the included charger or other compatible chargers. This allows you to quickly top up your battery when you're short on time.

- Charging Speeds: The Pixel 9 Pro XL boasts impressive charging speeds, potentially reaching up to 80W with a compatible charger. This means you can charge your phone from 0% to 100% in a significantly shorter time compared to standard charging.

Wireless Charging
- Qi Standard: The Pixel 9 Pro XL supports wireless charging using the Qi standard. This allows you to charge your phone by simply placing it on a compatible wireless charging pad.
- Fast Wireless Charging: Your Pixel also supports fast wireless charging with compatible wireless chargers. This provides faster charging speeds compared to standard wireless charging.
- Wireless Charging Speeds: The Pixel 9 Pro XL might support wireless charging speeds of up to 50W with a compatible charger.

Unique Charging Features
- Adaptive Charging: This feature learns your charging habits and optimizes charging speeds to prolong battery health. It might slow down charging

overnight to prevent overcharging and extend the lifespan of your battery.

- Battery Share: You can use your Pixel 9 Pro XL to wirelessly charge other devices, such as headphones or smartwatches, by enabling Battery Share in the settings.

Troubleshooting Tips

➤ Slow Charging Speeds: If you're experiencing slow charging speeds, make sure you're using a compatible charger and cable. Also, check that the charging port on your phone is clean and free of debris.

➤ Wireless Charging Issues: If you're having trouble with wireless charging, ensure that your phone is properly aligned on the wireless charging pad and that the pad is plugged in and receiving power. Also, check that your phone case isn't interfering with wireless charging.

Highlight: The Pixel 9 Pro XL's fast charging capabilities, both wired and wireless, ensure that you spend less time tethered to a charger and more time enjoying your phone. With its unique charging features and convenient options, your Pixel keeps you powered up and ready for action throughout your day.

Battery Saver and Adaptive Battery

The Google Pixel 9 Pro XL offers intelligent features like Battery Saver and Adaptive Battery to help you maximize your battery life and stay connected for longer. Whether you need to conserve power in a pinch or want to optimize battery usage over the long term, your Pixel has you covered.

Battery Saver Mode:

Battery Saver mode is a handy feature that helps you extend battery life when you're running low or anticipate needing your phone to last longer than usual.

Activating Battery Saver:

- Open Battery Settings: Go to Settings > Battery.
- Turn on Battery Saver: Tap on "Battery Saver" and toggle it on. You can also access Battery Saver from the Quick Settings panel in the notification shade.

How it Works: Battery Saver mode limits background activity, reduces visual effects, and restricts certain app functionalities to conserve power. You might notice some changes, such as:

- Darker Theme: The interface might switch to a darker theme to save power on OLED displays.
- Reduced Brightness: Screen brightness might be lowered.
- Limited Background Activity: Apps might not update in the background as frequently.
- Restricted Features: Some features, such as location services and automatic syncing, might be disabled or limited.

Customizing Battery Saver: You can customize Battery Saver settings to choose which features are restricted and set a battery percentage threshold for automatically activating Battery Saver.

Adaptive Battery:

Adaptive Battery is an AI-powered feature that learns your app usage patterns and optimizes battery consumption accordingly.

How it Works: Adaptive Battery identifies apps that you use frequently and prioritizes battery power for those apps. It also identifies apps that you rarely use and limits their background activity to conserve power.

- Enabling Adaptive Battery: Go to Settings > Battery > Adaptive Battery and toggle it on.

Tips to Extend Battery Life

While the Pixel 9 Pro XL boasts impressive battery life, there are always ways to optimize your usage and squeeze out even more power. Here are some practical tips to extend your battery life and keep your Pixel running longer:

Display and Brightness

- Dim the Lights: Lowering your screen brightness can significantly impact battery life. Adjust the brightness manually or enable Adaptive Brightness in Settings > Display > Brightness level to automatically optimize brightness based on ambient lighting.
- Shorter Screen Timeout: Reduce the screen timeout duration in Settings > Display > Screen timeout so your screen turns off sooner when not in use.
- Dark Mode: Embrace the dark side! Using dark mode can save battery, especially on phones with OLED displays like the Pixel 9 Pro XL, as black pixels are essentially turned off. Enable dark mode in Settings > Display > Dark theme.

Connectivity

- Wi-Fi over Mobile Data: When possible, connect to Wi-Fi networks instead of relying on mobile data, as Wi-Fi generally consumes less power.
- Airplane Mode: If you're in an area with no signal or don't need connectivity, enable Airplane Mode to disable all wireless connections.
- Bluetooth and Location Services: Turn off Bluetooth and location services when you're not using them to prevent unnecessary battery drain.

App Management

- Limit Background Activity: Restrict background activity for apps you don't use frequently. Go to Settings > Apps > See all apps, select the app, and toggle on "Restrict background data."
- Uninstall Unused Apps: Remove apps you no longer use to free up storage space and prevent them from consuming resources in the background.
- Update Apps: Keep your apps updated. App updates often include performance improvements and bug fixes that can optimize battery usage.

AUDIO AND MEDIA

Stereo Speakers and Audio Quality

The Google Pixel 9 Pro XL is designed to provide a rich and immersive audio experience, whether you're listening to music, watching videos, or playing games. Let's explore the quality of its stereo speakers and the technologies that enhance your listening pleasure.

Stereo Speaker Setup

The Pixel 9 Pro XL features a dual stereo speaker setup:

- Top Speaker: Located at the top of the phone, typically integrated into the earpiece.
- Bottom Speaker: Positioned at the bottom edge of the phone.

This dual speaker configuration creates a wider soundstage and delivers a more immersive audio experience compared to mono speakers.

Audio Quality

> Clarity and Detail: The Pixel 9 Pro XL's speakers are tuned to deliver clear and detailed audio with balanced highs, mids, and lows. You can enjoy crisp

vocals, rich instrumentals, and immersive sound effects.

> Loudness: The speakers are capable of producing a decent level of loudness, making them suitable for personal listening or sharing audio with a small group in a quiet environment.

Audio Enhancements: The Pixel 9 Pro XL might incorporate audio enhancement technologies, such as:

- Dolby Atmos: This technology creates a more immersive and spatial audio experience by simulating surround sound.
- Audio Tuning by [Audio Partner, e.g., Bose]: The speakers might be tuned by a renowned audio company like Bose to deliver a premium sound signature.

Potential Challenges

> Loudness Limitations: While the speakers offer decent loudness, they might not be sufficient for loud environments or large gatherings.

> Bass Response: The bass response might be limited due to the phone's compact size and speaker design.

Tips for Optimal Audio

- Speaker Placement: Pay attention to the placement of the speakers when holding the phone to avoid blocking them and muffling the sound.
- Volume Control: Adjust the volume to a comfortable level to avoid distortion or discomfort.
- Headphones for Enhanced Audio: For a more immersive and private listening experience, use headphones. The Pixel 9 Pro XL supports both wired headphones (via the USB-C port) and wireless headphones (via Bluetooth).

Dolby Atmos Support

The Google Pixel 9 Pro XL supports Dolby Atmos, an advanced audio technology that creates a more immersive and spatial sound experience. Whether you're watching movies, listening to music, or playing games, Dolby Atmos adds a new dimension to your audio, making you feel like you're in the center of the action.

Enabling Dolby Atmos

- ➢ Open Sound Settings: Go to Settings > Sound & vibration.

➤ Dolby Atmos: Look for the "Dolby Atmos" setting and tap on it.

Choose a Mode: You might have different Dolby Atmos modes to choose from:

- Automatic: Dolby Atmos will be automatically enabled for compatible content and headphones.
- Movie: Optimized for movies and TV shows.
- Music: Enhanced for music listening.
- Game: Immersive sound for gaming.

The Dolby Atmos Experience

➤ Spatial Audio: Dolby Atmos creates a sense of space and depth in audio, making it feel like sounds are coming from all around you, not just from your phone's speakers or headphones.

➤ Immersive Sound: Experience movies, music, and games with greater realism and immersion. You'll feel like you're in the middle of the action, with sounds moving around you and enveloping you in the experience.

➤ Enhanced Clarity: Dolby Atmos can also improve audio clarity and detail, making it easier to hear subtle sounds and nuances in your audio content.

Potential Challenges

- Compatible Content: Not all content is Dolby Atmos compatible. To experience the full benefits of

Dolby Atmos, you'll need to find content that supports it. Streaming services like Netflix and Amazon Prime Video offer a growing library of Dolby Atmos content.

- Compatible Headphones: While Dolby Atmos can work with your phone's built-in speakers, the experience is significantly enhanced with Dolby Atmos compatible headphones. These headphones are designed to deliver the spatial audio effects of Dolby Atmos.

Highlight: Dolby Atmos on the Pixel 9 Pro XL transforms your phone into a portable entertainment powerhouse, delivering an immersive audio experience that rivals home theater systems. Whether you're a movie buff, a music lover, or a gamer, Dolby Atmos adds a new dimension to your audio enjoyment.

Audio Settings and Customization

The Google Pixel 9 Pro XL offers a range of audio settings and customization options to help you tailor your sound experience to your preferences. Whether you want to boost the bass, enhance vocal clarity, or adjust the balance between left and right channels, your Pixel gives you the tools to fine-tune your audio.

Accessing Audio Settings

Open Sound Settings: Go to Settings > Sound & vibration.

Explore Audio Options: You'll find various audio settings, including:

- Media volume: Control the volume for media playback, such as music, videos, and games.
- Call volume: Adjust the volume for phone calls.
- Ringtone & notification volume: Set the volume for ringtones and notifications.
- Alarm volume: Control the volume for alarms.
- Haptic feedback: Adjust the intensity of vibrations for touch interactions.

Customizing Sound Profiles

- ➢ Sound modes: Your Pixel 9 Pro XL might offer different sound modes, such as "Music," "Movie," and "Game," each with its own pre-configured audio profile. You can switch between these modes to optimize the sound for different types of content.

Equalizer Settings

Adjusting the Equalizer: An equalizer allows you to fine-tune the audio frequencies to achieve your desired sound. You might find a built-in equalizer in the audio settings or within specific music apps.

- Frequency Bands: Equalizers typically have several frequency bands, such as bass, midrange, and treble. You can adjust the levels of each band to boost or reduce certain frequencies.
- Presets: Many equalizers offer presets, such as "Rock," "Pop," "Classical," and "Jazz," which apply pre-configured equalizer settings for different music genres.

Volume Balance

➢ Adjusting Balance: You can adjust the balance between the left and right audio channels to compensate for hearing differences or speaker placement. This setting is usually found in the accessibility settings or within specific audio apps.

Troubleshooting Tips

- Finding Audio Settings: If you're having trouble finding specific audio settings, try searching for them within the Settings app or checking the help documentation for your Pixel 9 Pro XL.

- Achieving Desired Sound: Experiment with different equalizer settings and sound profiles to find what sounds best to you. You can also try using third-party equalizer apps from the Google Play Store for more advanced audio customization options.

Connecting to Wireless Audio Devices

The Google Pixel 9 Pro XL embraces the freedom of wireless audio, allowing you to connect effortlessly to Bluetooth headphones, speakers, and other audio devices. Enjoy your music, podcasts, and audiobooks without the tangle of wires, whether you're at home, at the gym, or on the go.

Pairing with Bluetooth Audio Devices
Enable Bluetooth:

- Open Settings > Connected devices > Connection preferences > Bluetooth and toggle it on.

- Alternatively, swipe down from the top of the screen to open the notification shade, then tap the Bluetooth icon to turn it on.

Put Device in Pairing Mode:

- Make sure the Bluetooth audio device you want to connect to is in pairing mode. This usually involves pressing and holding a button on the device until an indicator light flashes. Refer to the device's instructions for specific pairing instructions.

Select Device on Your Pixel:

- On your Pixel 9 Pro XL, tap "Pair new device" under the Bluetooth settings.
- Your phone will scan for available devices. Select your desired audio device from the list.
- You might need to confirm the pairing on both your Pixel and the audio device.

Managing Connected Devices

- View Connected Devices: Go to Settings > Connected devices to see a list of currently connected Bluetooth devices.
- Disconnect: To disconnect from a device, tap on its name in the list and select "Disconnect."
- Forget Device: To remove a paired device, tap on its name and select "Forget." This will require you to

pair the device again if you want to connect to it in the future.

- Switch Between Devices: You can easily switch between connected audio devices by selecting the desired device from the list in the Bluetooth settings or from the media player's output options.

Potential Challenges

➤ Pairing Issues: If you're having trouble pairing with a device, make sure it's in pairing mode, is within range (usually around 30 feet), and has enough battery power. You can also try restarting your Pixel or the audio device.

➤ Audio Lag: Some Bluetooth devices might experience audio lag, especially when watching videos or playing games. This can be caused by interference or limitations of the Bluetooth connection. Try moving closer to the audio device or using a different Bluetooth codec (if supported) to minimize lag.

TROUBLESHOOTING AND UPDATES

Updating Software and Applications

Keeping your Google Pixel 9 Pro XL's software and apps up to date is crucial for optimal performance, security, and access to the latest features. Updates often include bug fixes, performance improvements, and new functionalities that enhance your mobile experience.

Updating Phone Software

Your Pixel 9 Pro XL will typically notify you when a software update is available. However, you can also manually check for updates:

- ➤ Open Settings: Go to Settings > System > System update.
- ➤ Check for Updates: Tap "Check for update" to see if any updates are available.
- ➤ Download and Install: If an update is available, tap "Download and install." It's recommended to connect to Wi-Fi before downloading updates to

avoid using mobile data and potentially incurring extra charges.

➤ Restart: Your phone will restart to apply the update. Make sure your phone is sufficiently charged before installing updates.

Updating Apps

Apps are typically updated through the Google Play Store.

➤ Open Play Store: Open the Google Play Store app.

➤ Manage Apps & Device: Tap on your profile picture in the top right corner and select "Manage apps & device."

Update Apps:

- Update All: Tap "Update all" to update all apps with available updates.

- Selective Updates: Tap "See details" to view available updates for individual apps. Select the apps you want to update and tap "Update."

Why Updates Matter

➤ Security: Security updates patch vulnerabilities that could be exploited by malware and other threats, protecting your phone and your data.

➤ Performance: Updates often include performance optimizations that make your phone faster and more efficient.

➤ New Features: Updates can introduce new features and functionalities, enhancing your mobile experience.

➤ Bug Fixes: Updates address bugs and glitches that might be affecting the performance or stability of your phone or apps.

Potential Challenges

● Delayed Updates: Some users might delay installing updates due to inconvenience or concerns about potential bugs. However, delaying updates leaves your phone vulnerable to security threats and can prevent you from accessing the latest features.

● Update Errors: Occasionally, errors might occur during the update process. If you encounter an error, try restarting your phone or clearing the cache for the Google Play Store (Settings > Apps > See all apps > Google Play Store > Storage & cache > Clear cache).

Highlight: Keeping your Pixel 9 Pro XL and its apps updated is essential for maintaining optimal security, performance, and functionality. By staying current with updates, you can enjoy a smooth, secure, and feature-rich mobile experience.

Automatic System and Security Updates

Staying up-to-date with the latest software and security patches is crucial for keeping your Google Pixel 9 Pro XL secure and running smoothly. Thankfully, your Pixel offers convenient options for enabling automatic updates, ensuring that your phone is always protected and equipped with the newest features.

Enabling Automatic System Updates

➤ Open Settings: Go to Settings > System > System update.

➤ Update Settings: Tap on the gear icon or the three dots in the top right corner to access update settings.

➤ Enable Automatic Updates: Look for the option to enable automatic updates. This will allow your Pixel to automatically download and install system updates when they're available, typically overnight or when your phone is connected to Wi-Fi and charging.

Customize Update Preferences: You might find options to customize your update preferences, such as:

- Download over Wi-Fi only: Restrict update downloads to Wi-Fi to avoid using mobile data.
- Schedule updates: Choose a preferred time for updates to be installed, such as overnight.

Enabling Automatic Security Updates

Security updates are typically included in system updates, but you might also find separate settings for automatic security updates.

- Open Security Settings: Go to Settings > Security.
- Find Security Update Settings: Look for a setting related to security updates or Google Play system updates.
- Enable Automatic Updates: Make sure the option to automatically install security updates is turned on.

Addressing Potential Challenges

- ➤ Disabled Automatic Updates: Some users might disable automatic updates due to concerns about data usage or potential disruptions. However, disabling automatic updates leaves your phone vulnerable to security threats and can prevent you from accessing the latest features and performance improvements.

➤ Data Usage: If you're concerned about data usage during updates, make sure the "Download over Wi-Fi only" option is enabled in the update settings.

Highlight: Enabling automatic updates for your Pixel 9 Pro XL's software and security patches is a simple yet crucial step in ensuring your phone remains secure, up-to-date, and performing at its best. By automating this process, you can enjoy peace of mind knowing that your Pixel is always protected and equipped with the latest features and enhancements.

Managing Device Performance

Your Google Pixel 9 Pro XL is designed for smooth and efficient performance, but over time, accumulated files, cached data, and running apps can slow it down. By proactively managing your device's resources, you can maintain optimal performance and ensure your Pixel continues to operate at its best.

Managing Storage

➤ Check Storage Usage: Go to Settings > Storage to see an overview of your storage usage. Identify which types of files are taking up the most space, such as photos, videos, apps, and audio files.

➤ Delete Unnecessary Files: Delete any files you no longer need, such as old photos, videos, documents, and downloaded files.

➤ Offload to Cloud Storage: Consider moving large files, such as photos and videos, to cloud storage services like Google Photos, Google Drive, or other cloud providers. This frees up space on your phone while keeping your files accessible.

➤ Uninstall Unused Apps: Remove apps you no longer use to free up storage space and prevent them from consuming resources in the background.

Clearing Cache

Cached data is temporary information that apps store to load content faster. However, over time, cached data can accumulate and take up valuable storage space.

- Clear App Cache: Go to Settings > Apps > See all apps, select the app, and tap "Storage & cache." Then, tap "Clear cache" to remove the app's cached data.

- Clear System Cache: You can also clear the system cache by going to Settings > Storage > Free up space.

Closing Unused Apps

Leaving apps running in the background can consume memory and processing power, potentially slowing down your phone.

- Close Recent Apps: Swipe up from the bottom of the screen and hold to view recent apps. Swipe up on an app's card to close it.
- Limit Background Processes: Go to Settings > Developer options (you might need to enable Developer options first) and limit the number of background processes allowed.

Other Performance Tips

➢ Restart Your Phone: A simple restart can often resolve performance issues by clearing temporary files and refreshing system processes.

➢ Keep Software Updated: Make sure your Pixel 9 Pro XL's software is up to date. Software updates often include performance optimizations and bug fixes.

➢ Avoid Extreme Temperatures: Extreme temperatures can affect performance. Avoid using your phone in direct sunlight or excessively hot or cold environments.

Highlight: By actively managing storage, clearing cache, closing unused apps, and following other performance tips, you can ensure your Pixel 9 Pro XL continues to deliver a smooth and responsive experience. Remember, a little maintenance goes a long way in keeping your Pixel running at its best.

MASTERING GOOGLE ASSISTANT

Activating & Using Google Assistant

The Google Pixel 9 Pro XL puts the power of Google Assistant at your fingertips, ready to assist you with a wide range of tasks, answer your questions, and provide information. Whether you need to set a reminder, send a message, play music, or control your smart home devices, Google Assistant is your ever-ready helper.

Activating Google Assistant

There are several ways to activate Google Assistant on your Pixel 9 Pro XL:

Voice activation:

- Say "Hey Google" or "Ok Google" to wake up Google Assistant.
- Make sure voice activation is enabled in Settings > Google > Google Assistant > Voice Match.

Squeeze the phone:

- If your Pixel supports Active Edge, squeeze the lower part of the phone to activate Google Assistant.

- You can customize Active Edge settings in Settings > System > Gestures > Active Edge.

Home button:

- Press and hold the home button to launch Google Assistant.

Swipe from corner:

- Swipe diagonally from either bottom corner of the screen to activate Google Assistant.

Using Google Assistant

Once Google Assistant is activated, you can ask questions, give commands, or make requests using natural language.

Here are some examples:

Basic commands:

- "Set an alarm for 7 AM."
- "Call Mom."
- "Send a message to John."
- "Play music by [artist name]."
- "What's the weather like today?"
- "Set a reminder to buy groceries."

Information retrieval:

- "What's the capital of France?"
- "How tall is Mount Everest?"
- "What's the latest news?"
- "Find restaurants near me."

Device control:

- "Turn on the lights."
- "Set the thermostat to 72 degrees."
- "Play Netflix on the living room TV."

Tips for Using Google Assistant

➤ Speak clearly: Speak clearly and at a moderate pace for better voice recognition.

➤ Use natural language: You can use natural language and full sentences when interacting with Google Assistant.

➤ Explore commands: Try different commands and queries to discover the full range of Google Assistant's capabilities.

➤ Customize settings: You can customize Google Assistant's settings, such as voice, language, and preferred responses, in the Google Assistant app.

Highlight: Google Assistant on the Pixel 9 Pro XL is a versatile and powerful tool that can simplify your life and enhance your mobile experience. By mastering its activation methods and exploring its capabilities, you can unlock a new level of convenience and efficiency.

Voice Commands and Queries

Google Assistant on your Pixel 9 Pro XL is ready to respond to your voice commands and queries, making it easier to perform tasks, get information, and control your digital world. Here's a list of useful voice commands to get you started:

Communication
Make Calls:
> "Call [contact name]."
> "Call [phone number]."
> "Make a video call to [contact name]."

Send Messages:
> "Send a text message to [contact name]."
> "Send a message to [contact name] on WhatsApp."
> "Send an email to [contact name]."

Check Notifications:
> "Read my notifications."
> "Do I have any new messages?"

Productivity
Set Alarms and Reminders:
> "Set an alarm for 7 AM."
> "Set a reminder to buy groceries at 5 PM."
> "Wake me up in 30 minutes."

Create Calendar Events:

- ➤ "Create a calendar event for tomorrow at 2 PM."
- ➤ "Add a meeting with [contact name] to my calendar."

Take Notes:

- ➤ "Take a note."
- ➤ "Note to self: [your note]."
- ➤ "Create a shopping list."

Set Timers:

- ➤ "Set a timer for 10 minutes."
- ➤ "Start a timer for cooking pasta."

Entertainment

Play Music and Podcasts:

- ➤ "Play music by [artist name]."
- ➤ "Play [song title]."
- ➤ "Play some jazz music."
- ➤ "Play my workout playlist on Spotify."
- ➤ "Play the latest episode of [podcast name]."

Control Media Playback:

- ➤ "Pause music."
- ➤ "Next song."
- ➤ "Volume up."
- ➤ "Rewind 30 seconds."

Find Videos:

> "Play [movie title] on Netflix."

> "Search YouTube for [topic]."

Information Retrieval

Get Weather Updates:

> "What's the weather like today?"

> "What's the temperature in Lagos?"

> "Will it rain tomorrow?"

Find Places:

> "Find restaurants near me."

> "Where is the nearest gas station?"

> "Get directions to [location]."

Get Answers:

> "What's the capital of Nigeria?"

> "How tall is Mount Kilimanjaro?"

> "What's the population of Lagos?"

Smart Home Control

Control Smart Home Devices:

> "Turn on the lights."

> "Set the thermostat to 25 degrees."

> "Lock the front door."

> "Turn off the TV."

Tips for Using Voice Commands

- Speak clearly: Speak clearly and at a moderate pace for better voice recognition.
- Use natural language: You can use natural language and full sentences when giving commands.
- Be specific: The more specific your command, the better Google Assistant will understand your request.
- Experiment: Try different commands and queries to discover the full range of Google Assistant's capabilities.

Routines and Automation with Google Assistant

Google Assistant on your Pixel 9 Pro XL can do more than just respond to individual commands; it can also automate entire routines with a single voice command or at a scheduled time. Imagine waking up to your favorite music, having the lights turn on, and getting a briefing of your day's agenda, all with a single "Good morning" command. That's the power of routines.

Creating Routines

Open Google Assistant Settings:

- Say "Hey Google, open Assistant settings."

- Alternatively, go to Settings > Google > Google Assistant.

Routines: Tap on "Routines."

Create a New Routine:

- Tap the plus button (+) to create a new routine.
- Alternatively, you can choose from pre-made routines and customize them.

Set the Trigger:

- Voice Command: Choose a voice command to trigger the routine, such as "Good morning," "Bedtime," or "I'm leaving."
- Time: Schedule the routine to start at a specific time, such as sunrise or sunset.

Add Actions:

Tap "Add action" to add actions to the routine. You can choose from a variety of actions, such as:

- Adjust device settings (brightness, volume, Do Not Disturb)
- Control smart home devices (lights, thermostat, locks)
- Play music or podcasts
- Provide information (weather, news, traffic)
- Communicate (send messages, make calls)
- Run other apps

Customize Order: Arrange the actions in the order you want them to occur.

Save the Routine: Tap "Save" to save your new routine.

Examples of Useful Routines

"Good Morning" Routine:

- Turn on the lights.
- Adjust the thermostat.
- Play your favorite morning playlist.
- Tell you the weather forecast and traffic conditions.
- Read your calendar appointments for the day.

"Bedtime" Routine:

- Turn off the lights.
- Set an alarm for the morning.
- Play relaxing music or white noise.
- Enable Do Not Disturb mode.

"I'm Leaving" Routine:

- Lock the doors.
- Turn off the lights.
- Set the thermostat to an energy-saving temperature.
- Play a podcast or audiobook for your commute.

Troubleshooting Routines

➢ Test Thoroughly: After creating a routine, test it thoroughly to ensure it works as expected.

- ➤ Check for Conflicts: If a routine isn't working, check for any conflicts with other routines or settings.
- ➤ Review Actions: Make sure the actions in the routine are configured correctly and that you have the necessary permissions granted.

Using Google Lens

Your Google Pixel 9 Pro XL comes equipped with Google Lens, a powerful tool that uses AI to understand what your camera sees. It can identify objects, translate text, search for information, and even help you shop for products online. Think of it as a visual search engine that unlocks a wealth of information about the world around you.

Activating Google Lens

There are several ways to activate Google Lens on your Pixel 9 Pro XL:

- ➤ From the Camera App: Open the Camera app and tap the Google Lens icon (it looks like a square with a dot in the center).
- ➤ From Google Photos: Open a photo in Google Photos and tap the Google Lens icon at the bottom of the screen.

➢ From Google Assistant: Activate Google Assistant and say "Open Google Lens" or tap the Google Lens icon in the Assistant interface.

Using Google Lens

Once Google Lens is activated, point your camera at the object or text you want to analyze. Google Lens will automatically try to identify what it sees and provide relevant information or actions.

Here are some examples of what you can do with Google Lens:

Identify Objects:

- Plants and Animals: Identify different species of plants and animals.
- Landmarks and Buildings: Learn more about famous landmarks and buildings.
- Products: Get information about products, such as reviews, prices, and where to buy them.

Translate Text:

- Real-time Translation: Point your camera at text in a foreign language, and Google Lens will translate it in real-time, overlaying the translation on the screen.
- Copy Text: Extract text from images and copy it to your clipboard.

Search for Information:

- Scan Barcodes and QR Codes: Scan barcodes and QR codes to quickly access product information or website links.
- Search by Image: Take a photo of an object and use it to search for information online.

Real-World Applications

- Shopping: Scan a product barcode to compare prices, read reviews, or find it online.
- Dining: Translate a menu in a foreign language or identify a dish you don't recognize.
- Travel: Learn more about landmarks and historical sites.
- Education: Identify plants and animals or get information about historical artifacts.
- Accessibility: Help people with visual impairments identify objects and navigate their surroundings.

Potential Challenges

- Camera Focus: Ensure your camera is properly focused on the object or text you want to analyze.
- Interpretation of Results: Google Lens might not always provide accurate or relevant results, especially for complex or ambiguous objects or text.
- Internet Connection: Google Lens requires an internet connection to function properly.

THE GOOGLE ECOSYSTEM

Connecting with Other Google Devices & Services

The Google Pixel 9 Pro XL seamlessly integrates with a wide range of Google devices and services, creating a connected ecosystem that enhances your digital life. From casting content to your TV with Chromecast to controlling your smart home with Google Home, and staying connected with a Wear OS watch, your Pixel becomes a central hub for a seamless and integrated experience.

Connecting to Chromecast

Chromecast allows you to wirelessly stream content from your Pixel 9 Pro XL to your TV or other displays.

> ➤ Set Up Chromecast: Plug your Chromecast device into your TV's HDMI port and follow the on-screen instructions to set it up.
> ➤ Connect to Wi-Fi: Ensure your Pixel 9 Pro XL and Chromecast are connected to the same Wi-Fi network.

➢ Cast Content: Open a compatible app, such as YouTube or Netflix, and tap the Cast icon. Select your Chromecast device to start streaming.

Connecting to Google Home

Google Home devices, such as smart speakers and displays, can be controlled with your Pixel 9 Pro XL.

➢ Set Up Google Home: Set up your Google Home device using the Google Home app.

➢ Link with Pixel: Make sure your Pixel 9 Pro XL is signed in to the same Google account as your Google Home device.

➢ Control with Voice or App: Use voice commands or the Google Home app on your Pixel to control your smart home devices, play music, get information, and more.

Connecting to Wear OS Watches

Wear OS smartwatches extend the functionality of your Pixel 9 Pro XL to your wrist.

➢ Pair with Watch: Enable Bluetooth on both your Pixel and your Wear OS watch. Open the Wear OS app on your Pixel and follow the on-screen instructions to pair the devices.

➢ Receive Notifications: Get notifications from your Pixel on your watch, such as calls, messages, and app alerts.

➢ Control with Watch: Use your watch to control music playback on your Pixel, track your fitness activities, and access Google Assistant.

Other Connections

- Pixel Buds: Connect to Pixel Buds or other Bluetooth headphones for a wireless audio experience.

- Chromebook: Seamlessly integrate your Pixel with a Chromebook to share files, access messages, and continue tasks across devices.

- Android Auto: Connect your Pixel to your car's infotainment system with Android Auto to access navigation, music, and communication features on your car's display.

Potential Challenges

➢ Connectivity Issues: If you encounter connectivity issues, ensure that your Pixel and the other device are connected to the same Wi-Fi network or have a stable Bluetooth connection. Restarting devices can also help resolve connectivity problems.

➤ Setup Difficulties: If you're having trouble setting up a connection, refer to the help documentation for the specific device or service.

Highlight: Connecting your Pixel 9 Pro XL with other Google devices and services creates a seamless and integrated ecosystem that enhances your digital life. By leveraging the power of this connected ecosystem, you can enjoy greater convenience, efficiency, and control over your technology.

Glossary

A

Android: The mobile operating system developed by Google that powers the Pixel 9 Pro XL.

App: Short for "application," a software program designed to perform a specific task on your phone.

Aspect Ratio: The proportional relationship between the width and height of an image or screen.

B

Bluetooth: A wireless technology that allows devices to connect and communicate with each other over short distances.

Brightness: The intensity of light emitted from a display screen.

C

Cache: Temporary data stored by apps and websites to speed up loading times.

Camera Sensor: The component in a camera that captures light and converts it into an image.

Cloud Storage: Storing data on remote servers accessed via the internet, rather than directly on your device.

D

Data Usage: The amount of data transmitted and received by your phone over a cellular network.

Display: The screen on your phone that shows visual content.

DPI (Dots Per Inch): A measure of pixel density, indicating how many pixels are present in one inch of a display.

E

Equalizer: A software tool that allows you to adjust audio frequencies to customize the sound profile.

F

Factory Reset: Restoring your phone to its original factory settings, erasing all data and customizations.

Fingerprint Sensor: A security feature that uses your unique fingerprint to unlock your phone.

Flash: A bright light on your phone that illuminates the scene when taking photos in low light.

Frame Rate: The number of frames (images) displayed per second in a video, affecting its smoothness.

G

Gesture Navigation: Controlling your phone using touch gestures, such as swiping and tapping.

Google Account: A user account that gives you access to Google services like Gmail, Drive, and Photos.

Google Assistant: A virtual assistant that responds to voice commands and provides information and assistance.

Google Play Store: The official app store for Android devices where you can download and install apps.

GPU (Graphics Processing Unit): A specialized processor that handles graphics rendering and visual tasks.

H

HDR+ (High Dynamic Range+): A camera feature that captures multiple exposures and combines them to create a photo with balanced highlights and shadows.

Home Screen: The main screen on your phone where you access app icons, widgets, and other features.

I

IP Rating: A standard that defines levels of sealing effectiveness against dust and water.

L

Latency: The delay between sending a request and receiving a response, especially in network communication.

Live Caption: A feature that automatically generates captions for audio playing on your phone.

M

Megapixel (MP): A unit of measurement for image resolution, representing one million pixels.

Mobile Data: Internet access provided by a cellular network, using your data plan.

Motion Mode: A camera mode that captures movement in creative ways, such as Action Pan and Long Exposure.

N

NFC (Near Field Communication): A short-range wireless technology used for contactless payments and data transfer.

Night Sight: A camera mode that captures bright and detailed photos in low-light conditions.

Notification Shade: The menu that appears when you swipe down from the top of the screen, showing notifications and quick settings.

O

OIS (Optical Image Stabilization): A camera technology that reduces blur caused by shaky hands.

P

Pixel Density: The number of pixels per inch (PPI) on a display, affecting image sharpness.

Processor (CPU): The "brain" of your phone that executes instructions and performs calculations.

R

RAM (Random Access Memory): Your phone's short-term memory, used to store actively running apps and data.

Resolution: The number of pixels that make up a display, affecting image clarity.

ROM (Read-Only Memory): Your phone's long-term memory, used to store the operating system and other essential files.

Routine: A set of actions that Google Assistant can perform automatically with a single voice command or at a scheduled time.

S

Screen Lock: A security feature that prevents unauthorized access to your phone.

SIM Card: A small card that identifies your phone on a cellular network.

Software Update: An update to your phone's operating system or apps that includes new features, bug fixes, and security enhancements.

Storage: The memory on your phone used to store apps, photos, videos, and other data.

T

Telephoto Lens: A camera lens that magnifies distant objects, allowing you to zoom in.

Theme: A set of visual elements that define the look and feel of your phone's interface.

Touchscreen: A display screen that responds to touch input.

U

Ultrawide Lens: A camera lens that captures a wider field of view than a standard lens.

USB-C: A type of connector used for charging and data transfer.

V

Viewfinder: The area on the camera screen that shows the live preview of what you're about to capture.

Voicemail: A service that allows callers to leave you a voice message when you're unavailable to answer a call.

W

Wallpaper: An image displayed as the background on your home screen or lock screen.

Widget: A mini-application that displays information or provides quick access to app features on your home screen.

Wi-Fi: A wireless technology that allows devices to connect to the internet.

FAQs

Q: How do I take a screenshot on my Pixel 9 Pro XL?

A: There are a couple of ways to capture a screenshot:

- Button combination: Press the Power button and the Volume Down button simultaneously.
- Quick Tap: If enabled, double-tap the back of your phone with Quick Tap. You can customize Quick Tap in Settings > System > Gestures > Quick Tap.

Q: How do I turn on the flashlight?

A: Swipe down from the top of the screen to open the notification shade. Then, tap the flashlight icon to turn it on or off.

Q: How do I check for software updates?

A: Go to Settings > System > System update and tap "Check for update."

Q: How do I extend my battery life?

A: There are several ways to save battery:

- Reduce screen brightness.
- Enable dark mode.
- Turn off unused features like Bluetooth and location services.
- Limit background app activity.
- Use Battery Saver mode.

Q: How do I connect to a Wi-Fi network?

A: Go to Settings > Network & internet > Internet, turn on Wi-Fi, and select your desired network from the list.

Q: How do I reset my phone to factory settings?
A: Caution: This will erase all data on your phone. Back up your important data before proceeding.

- Go to Settings > System > Reset options > Erase all data (factory reset).

Q: How do I use Google Pay for contactless payments?
A: First, make sure NFC is enabled in Settings > Connected devices > Connection preferences > NFC. Then, open the Google Pay app, add your cards, and follow the instructions to make contactless payments.

Q: How do I transfer files between my phone and computer?
A: Connect your phone to your computer using a USB-C cable. Select "File Transfer" or "MTP" on your phone when prompted. Then, use your computer's file explorer to access your phone's storage and transfer files.

Q: How do I use Google Assistant?
A: Say "Hey Google" or "Ok Google" to activate Google Assistant. You can then ask questions, give commands, or make requests using your voice.

Q: How do I turn on Do Not Disturb mode?

A: Swipe down from the top of the screen to open the notification shade. Then, tap the Do Not Disturb icon to turn it on or off. You can customize Do Not Disturb settings in Settings > Sound & vibration > Do Not Disturb.

Q: How do I clear my browsing history in Chrome?

A: Open the Chrome app, tap the three dots in the top right corner, and select "History." Then, tap "Clear browsing data" and choose the data you want to clear.

Q: How do I change the default app for a specific action (e.g., web browser, email app)?

A: Go to Settings > Apps > Default apps and select the category you want to change. Then, choose your preferred app from the list.

Q: Where can I find more help and support for my Pixel 9 Pro XL?

A: You can find online support resources, troubleshooting guides, and community forums on the Google Pixel website. You can also contact Google Support directly for personalized assistance.